IRREGULAR

OUR LIFE TOGETHER

A Woman's Workshop on Fellowship

Books in this series—

Our Life Together

A Woman's Workshop on Fellowship

With Leader's Guide

Lawrence O. Richards

ZONDERVAN
PUBLISHING HOUSE

OF THE ZONDERVAN CORPORATION
GRAND RAPIDS, MICHIGAN 49506

OUR LIFE TOGETHER: A WOMAN'S WORKSHOP ON FELLOWSHIP
© 1981 by The Zondervan Corporation

Unless indicated otherwise, Scripture quotations are from the Holy Bible: New International Version, © 1978 by the New York International Bible Society.

Library of Congress Cataloging in Publication Data
Richards, Larry, 1931–
    Our life together, a woman's workshop on fellowship.

    1. Christian life—1960–   . I. Title.
BV4501.2.R5124   248.8'43   81-11546
ISBN 0-310-43451-3   AACR2

Edited and designed by Mary Bombara

Printed in the United States of America

83 84 85 86 87 88 — 10 9 8 7 6 5 4 3 2

CONTENTS

1

A VERY PERSONAL COMMITMENT

I remember what a struggle it was.

I was brought up in a Christian home, and had always assumed that God was real and that the Bible was His Word. My parents' faith was accepted; it was just part of the way the world was.

Then, in the Navy, I found that believing what my mom and dad believed wasn't enough. I was busy in those days. I was stationed in New York city and enjoyed all the free movies, plays, and sports events that were available to servicemen through USO centers. But the activities and doing things with my friends did *not* satisfy. Something important was missing from my life, and I felt empty, though I didn't know why.

For years my mother had been reading a magazine called *Revelation* and listening to Donald Grey Barnhouse a then popular radio preacher. He had a Bible class in a Lutheran church in Manhattan on Monday nights. For some reason I went one evening, and for the first time was struck by the fact that what I had always accepted actually was *true*.

I began going to the class regularly. (Not every week, because sometimes I wouldn't get by the triple features on

Forty-second street.) And I began to get up early and walk up the eight flights of stairs to my office to study the Bible. Up there, in the old Brooklyn warehouse that housed the headquarters of the Military Sea Transport Command, I had my struggle. It wasn't that I didn't believe what I read. I did believe it. It was just that believing didn't seem to be *enough*.

I argued with God those mornings. "I've always believed this, Lord," I'd say. "It wouldn't be honest for me to pretend I'm not a believer. And You say that a person who believes on the Lord Jesus Christ shall be saved. How can I feel so uncertain about being a Christian when I honestly do believe?"

Finally I stopped struggling. One morning, on the eighth floor of our building, looking out over New York harbor, I simply told the Lord, "All right, God. If I've never trusted Christ as savior before, I do now." And the struggle was over.

My beliefs didn't change. But my relationship with God did. In my own mind at least, I stopped counting on the fact that I had always believed the right things about God and simply committed myself to Him, personally.

Christianity had stopped being a set of doctrines that I believed. It had become a very real and personal relationship.

Commitment

As I grew in my Christian life I learned a little more of what that moment of decision involved. I learned that it meant a mutual commitment—on my part and on God's!

Paul talked about each of these commitments in his New Testament letters. In Romans Paul caught the wonder and awe that come when I realize that, in Christ, God is totally committed to me. After recounting what God has done for us, Paul said,

> What, then, shall we say in response to this? If God is for us, who can be against us? He who did not spare his own Son, but gave him up for us all—how will he not also, along with him,

graciously give us all things? Who will bring any charge against those whom God has chosen? It is God who justifies. Who is he that condemns? Christ Jesus, who died—more than that, who was raised to life—is at the right hand of God and is also interceding for us. . . . I am convinced that neither death nor life, neither angels nor demons, neither the present nor the future, nor any powers, neither height nor depth, nor anything else in all creation, will be able to separate us from the love of God that is in Christ Jesus our Lord (Rom. 8:31–34, 38–39).

God's commitment is complete and personal. He has committed Himself to love me, always. No matter what.

This is hard to grasp. Like all human beings, I have a tendency to want to put my relationship with God on a business-like basis. That is, I want to feel that God loves me *because* I do the right things or *because* I believe in a particular set of truths. But this is not how personal commitment works. Personal commitment is an "always" and an "in spite of" kind of thing. True, we're loved when we do the things that please God. We're loved when we believe the truths revealed in the Scriptures. But, because of Jesus, we are loved *even when we do not choose to do what pleases God, and even when our doctrinal understanding is imperfect.* "Who dares condemn?" Paul asked. "Jesus Christ, who died—more than that, who was raised to life—is at the right hand of God, and is also interceding for us."

God *has committed Himself to me.* God *is for me.* His allegiance to me in Christ is total and complete.

This fact has tremendous implications when we think about our relationships with others. We have a tendency to impose conditions on our welcome to other Christians. They must believe or act as we do to be accepted.

Do we doubt tongues? Then, to be accepted by us a charismatic must deny his gift. Or, do we insist that tongues is a necessary experience today? Then a noncharismatic is unwelcome.

Do we consider drinking a sin? Then a person who keeps beer or wine in his refrigerator, even though he professes Christ as savior, is an outcast, as far as we are concerned.

But God isn't like this. When we trust ourselves to Jesus, God makes a full commitment of Himself to us. He is for us. He loves us. In fact, nothing in all creation can separate us from the love of God that is in Christ Jesus our Lord. His commitment to us is a deeply personal one. And, as we'll see later in this study, our commitment to each other is to be modeled on His example.

We need to learn to love each other *in spite of*. We need to learn to love each other *anyway*. That is God's kind of love, and God's kind of commitment.

My Commitment

The very personal commitment at the heart of Christianity is a mutual one. God commits Himself to me. And I commit myself to Him. He gives me His love. I give Him my full allegiance.

That word *allegiance* is an important one and it will play a vital role in our understanding of Christian fellowship. Probably one of the best synonyms for allegiance is "loyalty." My part of the relationship with God that I entered some 28 years ago is one of loyalty to Him.

The apostle Paul understood the problem of divided loyalties all too well. In his own experience he tended to equate loyalty to God with commitment to a set of beliefs or practices. He wrote:

> If anyone else thinks he has reasons to put confidence in the flesh, I have more: circumcised the eighth day, of the people of Israel, of the tribe of Benjamin, a Hebrew of Hebrews; in regard to the law, a Pharisee; as for zeal, persecuting the church; as for legalistic righteousness, faultless (Phil. 3:4–6).

Paul's lineage, his beliefs, his actions, even his zeal to serve God were beyond reproach. What was wrong? Paul explained that in all his loyalty to *religion* he did not know God personally, and so his allegiance was not to a person. It is relationship with God as a person and allegiance to Him that is the open secret of Christian faith.

> Whatever was to my profit I now consider loss for the sake of Christ. What is more, I consider everything a loss compared to the surpassing greatness of knowing Christ Jesus my Lord. . . . I consider them rubbish, that I may gain Christ and be found in him. . . . I want to know Christ and the power of his resurrection and the fellowship of sharing in his sufferings (Phil. 3:7–10).

This is something I didn't understand until later. I found out that some people would insist I conform to their doctrines, to their practices, or to their ideas of serving God. They would tell me *this* was Christianity.

But somehow I sensed from the beginning that my commitment and loyalty had been given to Jesus, personally. That my loyalty to Him could not be equated with—the doctrines of my church, the lists of "do's" and "don'ts" others hold as convictions, or the ideas others have of how God is to be served. My allegiance is given to Jesus personally, and He is the one I want to be loyal to.

This does not mean that I have no doctrinal position or hold no convictions. Not at all. But it does mean that I refuse to confuse my doctrines and my convictions with Jesus Himself.

Keeping the focus of loyalty on Jesus Himself is important in our relationships with other Christians. Because we are human beings and are fallible, we will have different ideas about doctrines and different ideas about practices as well. People who honestly seek to be loyal to Jesus will disagree with me.

If I confuse Christianity with loyalty to my doctrines or to my convictions, I'll have no way to accept my fellow Christians when we differ.

But Christianity isn't summed up on my fallible understandings or in my convictions. Christianity is summed up in Jesus Himself, the Son of God, who loved me and gave Himself for me. My own relationship with God is focused on Him, so that he is the one I am committed to be loyal to.

A part of that loyalty is expressed by applying my understanding of the Bible to my way of life. But I realize that I can make mistakes in both areas, and I trust God to love me in spite of such mistakes for He has committed Himself to me.

And now I have to give my fellow Christians that same right to be wrong. I have to give them the freedom to focus their loyalty on Jesus, and not demand that they be loyal to what I believe or to what I do.

Fellowship With God

The word *fellowship* is a deeply meaningful one in the Bible. It's the translation of a Greek word that means "sharing." Those who have fellowship with each other share with each other.

We share our experiences.

We share our feelings.

We share our thoughts.

We share material possessions.

We share ourselves.

So when the apostle John wrote about "fellowship with God" and about "fellowship with each other," he was speaking of a personal relationship in which there is an intimate sharing between persons.

"We proclaim to you what we have seen and heard," John said, putting relationship immediately on an experiential level, "so that you may have fellowship with us. And our

fellowship is with the Father and with his Son, Jesus Christ"
(1 John 1:3).

This is the true secret of that very personal commitment that
I made after years of believing the right things about God, but
not knowing Him personally. When I first trusted myself to
Jesus there was a sudden *sharing of life*, which has grown
ever since.

God made a commitment to me.

He committed Himself to love me: always and anyway.

I committed myself to God.

I committed my allegiance to Jesus, to be loyal to Him,
personally.

Every person who has made that step of faith and has entered a personal relationship with God through Jesus has
come into just this kind of fellowship—a fellowship of mutual
sharing and self giving. God has given Himself to be *for* me. I
have given myself to love and be loyal to Him.

And this, John teaches, is the basis for our fellowship with
other Christians! We and they have made the same kind of
commitment to God and have received the same kind of
commitment from God. God loves them now. He is for them.
And they seek to be loyal to Jesus. On this basis I can build a
sharing relationship with all other Christians, even when we
have differences in doctrine or convictions. What we share
together is so important that our differences no longer matter
much.

Very Very Personal

Long before I ever began to think about the kind of relationship I'd want to build with other believers, I had to deal with
that question that troubled me so much in New York.

I had believed the right things. I had lived a "good" kind of
life. But down deep I knew there was something missing.
Something that couldn't be summed up in what I believed or

didn't believe or in what I did and did not do. What I needed was to be sure of my own personal relationship with God.

That is something that no one else can judge about us—but we can examine it ourselves.

Have we committed ourself to Jesus, personally? Have we accepted His love for us and become comfortable in the assurance of His unconditional care?

Have we given Him our loyalty and so desire to grow to know Him better?

If so, then God has shared Himself with us, and we can share ourself with Him. If so, we have a firm foundation on which to build meaningful personal relationships with all others who share, as we do, fellowship with God.

Discovery 1

1. Read 1 John 1:1–4. The apostle John speaks about life together and uses the term *fellowship*. What does this word mean? (Feel free to use a dictionary.) _____

_____

_____

_____

_____

2. How important is personal experience with God to the relationship John is eager to share with others? Why do you believe it is important? _____

_____

_____

_____

_____

_____

3. Jot down memories of one experience with God which is especially significant to you. Describe it here in just a few words or phrases. _____

_____

_____

_____

4. Divide into small groups of six or eight persons. Share with each other the experience you just recalled and described. As you share, be sure to communicate your feelings as well as thoughts about it, and any long-term impact the experience has had in your life.

Then as the others share, jot down notes about each one which will help you in coming to know each person better.

5. Close in prayer in your group. Thank God for each other and how He is working in each life.

2

WELCOME HOME!

When I made that very personal commitment to Jesus, I entered into a very special relationship with God. What I didn't know then was that at the same time I had entered a special relationship with other Christians.

For a long time I couldn't sort that relationship out or understand it. It was enough for me to join a small Baptist church in Brooklyn. I knew I belonged there: they cared for me, and I cared for them, and we were the same. And that was very important to me.

But, at the same time I was at home with my little circle of friends in our local church, I wasn't really comfortable with other Christians. We Baptists had our distinctives: things that made us different from other people and from other Christians. We believed in baptism by immersion for those who had become Christians. We also believed in witnessing, and people in our church were expected to pass out tracts or tell others about salvation in very verbal and specific ways. And we believed in separation: our members didn't smoke or go to movies or drink any alcoholic beverages.

These differences were very important to us, and we didn't

feel comfortable with others who claimed to be Christians unless they shared those distinctives with us.

Professing allegiance to Jesus wasn't enough. Others had to share our distinctives as well as our relationship with the Lord in order for us to feel comfortable with them.

Defining by Differences

We all have a tendency to define ourselves and others on the basis of our differences. After all, there *are* differences between persons: very real ones. Some people are white, and others are black. Some are male, and others are female. Some are rich, and others are poor. Some are highly intelligent, and others, like my daughter Joy, are mentally retarded. Some people are married, and some are single. Some are young people, and others are old.

All these differences exist, and in fact there is nothing wrong with any of them. It's perfectly acceptable to be a young black married male. And it is perfectly acceptable to be an older white unmarried female. Each person is made in the image of God: each one has worth and value and is loved by Him. None of the differences change the fact that the individual is a human being and, as a human being, is of value to God.

We get into trouble when we start making differences *the* important thing about our identity. When I try to find my identity, for instance, in the fact that I am single and begin to feel uncomfortable with all marrieds, then I've missed something important. Or when I insist that my identity is summed up in my being a liberated woman (or a chauvinistic male), then I've missed what is really important.

It's the same thing in my relationship with other Christians: when I feel that others belong only if we share the same distinctives, then I'm missing what is really important about Christianity. When I feel that I can belong only with others who are Baptist—witnessing Christians who do not go to movies or drink—then I have become confused about what is basic. Or if I feel I can only belong with other Catholic charismatics, then I am missing what is central.

I do need to be clear about my identity. But I need to take my understanding of my identity from God's understanding of it, clearly focusing on what He says is basic and important.

What Is Important?

The apostle Peter gives us insight into our true identity in this exhortation in his first letter. "Now that you have purified yourselves by obeying the truth so that you have a sincere love for your brothers," he said, "love one another deeply, from the heart" (1 Peter 1:22). Peter called our commitment to Jesus being "born again," and urges us "like newborn babes" to grow up in our salvation (1 Peter 1:23; 2:2). The whole picture, even the language, is that of *family*. Given new life when God shared Himself with us, we entered a new world, and in that new world we have a new family! We have God Himself as our Father! And we have all other Christians as our brothers and sisters!

Paul, too, wanted us to think in family terms. In one prayer he spoke of kneeling "before the Father, from whom his whole family in heaven and on earth derives its name" (Eph. 3:14–15). What name do we take from God? Why, since He is Father, we Christians take our name—our identity—as *family* from our shared relationship with Him.

This is vitally important. Over and over in the New Testament the words *brother* and *sister* occur. Over and over we are called on to love one another and build the kind of relationships that are appropriate to a family. "You are now all sons of God through faith in Christ Jesus," Paul said in Galatians. If I have faith in Jesus, I am His child—I'm in His family. And anyone else who has faith in Jesus is also His child—part of His family with me.

Immediately Paul explained what this means. "There is neither Jew nor Greek, slave nor free, male nor female, for you are all one in Christ Jesus" (Gal. 3:28). Do you see what he's saying? There were still cultural differences between Jewish and Greek believers. There was a vast social chasm between slaves and free men. And there were greater differences then than there are now between males and females. The differences *existed.* But the *differences were no longer important!* They had been swallowed up in a great new reality! In Jesus each believer is a child of God, and thus the basic identity that each Christian shares is that of brother or sister in the one family of God the Father.

Now, it would be foolish to suggest that there are no significant differences of denomination, of doctrine, of practice, of ways of worship, of personal conviction. These differences do exist and probably always will exist. But the good news is that these differences are no longer important as far as fellowship is concerned! They too have been swallowed up in the new reality. In Jesus each believer is my brother or my sister. What we have in common is family. What we have in common is belonging to each other because we belong to God.

Belonging

Think about it for a minute. My wife and I have three children, who are all very different. Paul, the oldest, is married now. He is a very fine artist—a painter. He's also a body builder. At 5'11" and 215 pounds he can press over 500 pounds.

Tim is a senior in high school. He is taller and slimmer than Paul. He hasn't decided what he wants to become yet, but he has many talents and a particularly sharp philosophical mind.

Joy is eighteen and in a special school–home in Kentucky. She was brain damaged at birth and, although a loving and attractive person, she will always have to live in a sheltered community of some kind.

Oh, they're different, all right. They differ in physical appearance. In sex. In intellectual capacity. In personality. But each one is loved and each one belongs. Each is so confident of his or her acceptance that each one loves the others, even when their differences create friction.

This is what being a family is all about. It is belonging to each other in spite of differences. It's loving each other, even when differences create friction. It's the existence of an unbreakable bond that is ours because we share the life passed on to us by our parents.

It's the same with God's family. All of us in it are linked together by an unbreakable bond that is ours because we share the life passed on to us by God the Father in Jesus Christ. Linked in this way we belong to each other in spite of differences. Linked in this way we can love each other even when our differences create friction.

Building a Family Relationship

Peter said it in that verse we looked at earlier. Now that you "have a sincere love for your brothers, love one another deeply from the heart" (1 Peter 1:22).

I can look at another person who professes allegiance to Jesus and affirm "I love you." That is, I can intellectually accept the fact that he or she is family and thus is to be loved. I can even agree with God that, as His children, we are "all one in Christ Jesus." But Peter has added this phrase: "love one another deeply from the heart." So I realize that as one of God's family I am called by Him to *actively* come to know and love my brothers and sisters.

Now, it's clear that a determination to actively love my brothers and sisters in Christ doesn't mean that I'll try to know every Christian in the world or even every Christian in my community. There are just too many of us.

What, then, are the practical implications of *active* family love?

An attitude of openness. This is the first thing. I need to be open to building a relationship with any brother or sister the Lord brings into contact with me.

Back in my early days as a Christian I just wasn't open to others. I felt duty bound to make sure they were Baptists, that they were true Bible believers, holding the doctrines our church held. And then that they had the same list of "do's" and "don'ts" that I had. I had to probe and make sure that we were the same in our differences before I was comfortable trying to be friends, to say nothing of welcoming them as family.

But agreeing with God that everyone who has allegiance to Jesus is to be affirmed as brother or sister totally reversed that old attitude. Now I'm willing to be open and to share myself because I see the basic identity of others as children of God, and therefore as my brother or sister. I can face the fact that we may have differences from each other and say "I love you," anyway.

When I no longer classify others as "Catholic" or "Baptist" or "Calvinist" or "charismatic" or "neo-orthodox" or "fundamentalist," but see them in the basic identity they have in Christ as God's family, I have begun to develop an outlook that will free me to actively love others.

An aggressive approach. Perhaps aggressive isn't the best word. A better one might be "initiative-taking."

What I'm getting at is that many of us hang back, waiting for others to take the lead. We're lonely. But we don't go up to anyone and introduce ourselves. We notice another person who looks unhappy, but we hesitate to step up and ask, "Can I help?"

We live in a culture where isolation from others is a way of life—where superficial friendliness that never gets beneath the surface of life is the veneer spread over most interpersonal relationships. It's no wonder that we hesitate to take initiative in getting to know other Christians personally.

But being family does mean getting to know each other as persons. Loving one another deeply, as Peter exhorted, means developing close personal relationships. So we have to take initiative, and reach out for closer relationships with our Christian brothers and sisters.

A good place to start is within your own congregation. The Bible has a lot to say about hospitality. This is a very simple way to take initiative. Invite over for an evening a person or a couple in your congregation that you'd like to get to know. Call an acquaintance and go shopping together. Meet for lunch. Simply say, "I'd really like to get to know you better."

You can take the same kind of initiative with brothers and sisters you meet on your job or in your neighborhood. They may not go to your church. But, remember, that is not an important difference. What is important is that in Christ you are family.

Becoming part of a small group that meets weekly to share and to grow in allegiance to Jesus is one of the best ways to learn to be family. As you spend time together, come to know each other, and express to each other your own commitments to Christ, that "family" relationship, in which love is very real, will grow deeper.

Express affection. This is important in any family. And there are so many ways to say "I love you."

Of course, expressing love in words is one very important way. A welcoming smile and an "I'm so glad to see you!" tells a person he or she is loved. The touch of a hand, listening and entering into joy or sorrows can be an unmistakable expression of love. It's this kind of open expression of affection that Paul was speaking of in Romans when he said, "Greet one another with a holy kiss." Today we might say, "Give one another welcoming hugs!"

But letting others know you care for them as brothers and sisters goes beyond words. Concerning material needs John said, "If anyone has material possessions and sees his brother in need but has no pity on him, how can the love of God be in him? Dear children, let us not love with words or tongue but with actions and in truth" (1 John 3:17–18).

John was not speaking about communism or even commune living. He was simply letting us know that as we grow together as God's family, we find many ways to express the reality of the love that God gives us for each other. The loan of a car. Meals brought in when there is sickness. The quiet payment of a hospital bill. Help in finding a job. A ride to the store when your car is in the shop. All these are actions that flow out of deepening love for others in the family and that express love to them.

Not a New Legalism

Let's not misunderstand. The family relationship that grows between Christians when they love each other actively isn't a legalistic or an "ought to" kind of thing.

We start with an attitude of openness toward our fellow Christians: with the conviction that it is our shared membership in God's family and not our differences that are important. We go on, tentatively at first, to reach out and come to know others as persons. We take the initiative and build closer relationships. And then, as we share each other's lives, we find ourselves caring. Really caring!

We're glad to see each other. We want to have a part in joys and sorrows. And if someone we love is hurting or if they have a need, it's the most natural thing in the world to want to help.

God doesn't *demand* that we help. It's just that the growing love we feel within the family moves us to want to help. "Let us love one another," John says, "for love comes from God. . . . Since God so loved us, we also should love one another. No one has ever seen God, but if we love each other, God lives in us and his love is made complete in us" (1 John 4:7, 11–12).

One Christmas, our daughter Joy came to visit us from Kentucky. I met her at the airport. Rushing out of the corridor leading from the plane, she looked around eagerly, saying over and over again, "Daddy!" Then she saw me. With a squeal of delight she ran to me and threw herself in my arms.

Laughing and crying, we hugged. Joy was welcome. Joy was home.

This is our Good News as God's children. Wherever we are there are warm arms to hug us, warm welcomes awaiting us.

Where *you* are, all around you, there is *family*. So let down the barriers. Reach out. And find the brothers and sisters God has given you. Love, and be loved. Experience God's own warm "welcome home" through the brothers and sisters He has provided to be family to you.

Discovery 2

1. Recall a relationship with others in which you had a deep sense of belonging. Take a few minutes to share this with one other person, to tell her about that relationship and then to listen to her share.

2. List together all the traits that you can think of that describe a "good family." _____

_____

_____

_____

_____

3. Have one person read aloud the "What *Is* Important" section of this chapter. Then discuss the following questions together:

    a. What makes us members of God's family?

    b. What is our relationship with other members of His family?

    c. How can we build a "family" relationship with brothers and sisters with whom we may disagree?

4. Divide into groups of four. Have each group choose one of the three chapter suggestions on building a family relationship (either an attitude of openness, an "aggressive" approach, or expressing affection). Reread this section in the chapter and then list at least twenty things a person applying this principle might do to help build a family feeling with others in the family of God.

_____   _____

_____   _____

_____   _____

_____   _____

_____   _____

_____   _____

5. Come together and let each group share its ideas for applying these principles in daily life.

6. Close in prayer, thanking God specifically for others in your study group. Rejoice that they are members with you of His family.

3

WHAT I HAVE, I GIVE

One of the most wonderful things about being a member of God's family is the sense of belonging that comes as I grow to love my brothers and sisters. Another wonder is this: I suddenly discover that I am needed!

Most of us have been forced to question our significance. Only a few of us are what the world calls "successful." Even fewer are famous. But what hurts more than this is the feeling that even in the circle of my own small community of family and friends, I may not seem to count for much.

This especially hurts when, as a Christian, I want to serve the Lord—when my personal commitment to Jesus cries out to be expressed and I *need* to have my life count.

Most Christians think of "significance" in terms of some kind of service through their church. To them, ministers are significant. And radio or TV preachers. Or congregational leaders, who are looked to with respect because of some official position. But most of us can't be preachers or missionaries. Many of us would never feel comfortable heading a committee, or even teaching a Sunday school class.

And so for many Christians the feeling of being important to others—of really counting—is out of the question. Or is it?

Does it make a difference if we look at other Christians as family? Is there a *personal importance* we can have in God's family that we might never have if Christ's church were just a fine institution?

From a look into the Bible, it's clear that there *is* a difference. When we learn to relate to other Christians in a family, brother-and-sister way, we find a whole new basis for personal significance. We discover that we truly are important to God—and to others!

You might think of it this way. In your home, is your family organized into committees? Is one person more important than another because of the office he or she holds? If yours is like most families, you have no formal organization at all. You simply live together. As you live together, you each make whatever contribution you can to the growth and experience of each other.

While God's family is obviously larger (and while local churches may need organization and offices and all the trappings of an institution), it is important to keep in mind that we Christians are always, first and foremost, family. In God's family, too, the most significant contributions we make to others' lives are made through relationships, not through official "positions" at all. Looking into the Bible, we make the exciting discovery that people are what is really important to God and that each one of us is called in our relationships with others in God's family to build people!

What God Cares About Is People

The apostle Paul had that fact clearly in mind when he wrote to the Thessalonians, "What is our hope our joy, or the crown in which we will glory in the presence of our Lord Jesus when he comes? Is it not you? Indeed, you are our glory and our joy" (1 Thess. 2:19–20).

Peter has reminded us that "the heavens will disappear with a roar; the elements will be destroyed by fire, and the earth and everything in it will be laid bare" (2 Peter 3:10). When everything in the physical universe is destroyed in this way, what will remain? Only human beings, who have been gifted by God with a life that goes on forever and forever.

No wonder God cares about people so much! All the great church buildings erected by famous men will dissipate in a blast of heat. All the copies of the books of the most famous authors will disappear. Only people will be left. No wonder Paul said to the Thessalonians that they are his joy, and that their lives are what he will glory in when Jesus comes.

Actually, the Bible paints a beautiful picture of what we will be like when Jesus comes. "Dear friends," John said, "now we are children of God, and what we will be has not yet been made known. But we know that when he [Jesus] appears, we shall be like him, for we shall see him as he is" (1 John 3:2).

Over and over in the New Testament we see the promise. We are destined to be like Jesus (*see* Rom. 8:29; 8:16–19; 1 Cor. 15:49). God has committed himself to work in our lives and to bring us finally to Jesus' own likeness.

But growth and change and progress toward Jesus' likeness isn't something that God puts off until the Second Coming. Oh no. God has already begun the process! We "are being transformed into his [Jesus'] likeness with ever-increasing glory, which comes from the Lord, who is the Spirit" (2 Cor. 3:18). This exciting personal renewal helps us shake off the old and sinful patterns that may have infected our personalities—like bitterness, rage, anger, envy, and such. By God's renewal we are freed to become more and more kind, compassionate, forgiving, and loving—to be like Jesus. The Bible talks of this as being "made new in the attitude of your minds; and to put on the new self, created to be like

God in true righteousness and holiness" (Eph. 4:23–24).

When we think about becoming like Jesus, and about being part of God's family now, it's really not surprising. After all, children are expected to be like their parents. It's only natural that we should grow in family resemblance to our Father, God. And this is just how Jesus put it in Matthew. He was talking to His followers and was saying that we are to love our enemies. We're to pray for those who persecute us. And then he explained: this is so that we will be "sons of our Father in heaven." Then Jesus continued, "He causes his sun to rise on the evil and the good, and sends rain on the righteous and the unrighteous" (Matt. 5:43–48).

We are to be like our Father and like Jesus. We are to bear the family resemblance. We can summarize it this way:

- Each member of God's family is on a journey.
- That journey takes each one of us nearer and nearer to Christlikeness.
- Each of us and our progress on your journey is vitally important to God.

Why Christlikeness?

Some Christians are disturbed when the journey toward Christlikeness is emphasized. They feel that this teaching sounds selfish—as if God only cares about His own family and not the rest of the world.

It's true that God does have a very special love for you as His child. So what happens to you *is* on God's heart. He desires that you and I experience His very best. But this isn't a selfish or even a self-centered point of view. Just the opposite!

The Bible makes it clear that God cares about all people. He wants each one to respond to His love. He cares about society. He wants to see justice established. He cares about the poor. He wants to see suffering and sorrow relieved. He cares about the homeless and the sick. He yearns to see them comforted and healed.

But how is God going to communicate His love to the lost? How is He going to speak out for justice, or care for the poor? Right! *He is going to work through His family!*

This is why it's so important that you and I and our brothers and sisters all grow toward Christlikeness. The more we are like Jesus, the more we will love the lost and reach out to them. The more we are like Jesus, the more angry we will be over injustice. The more we are like Jesus, the more we will suffer with the poor and act to relieve them. The more we are like Jesus, the more we will hurt with the hurting and bring healing.

One well-known song suggests that God could have written "I love you" across the skies and still we would have remained unconvinced. How did we grasp the reality of God's love? Only by God's sending of His Son, who became a human being, lived among us, and ultimately died for us. We recognized love when love was incarnated in the person of Jesus Christ.

This is one of the great purposes of Christlikeness. Jesus today takes on flesh-and-blood expression in the lives of His brothers and sisters! This is exactly what the Bible says when it speaks of believers as "letters from Christ" written by the "Spirit of the living God" (2 Cor. 3:3). As we are transformed into Jesus' likeness, Christ walks the earth again in us. Just as Jesus communicated God's own love and compassion and goodness in Palestine some two thousand years ago, today Jesus expresses himself through our transformed personalities.

So we want to add this to our summary:

- Each member of God's family is on a journey.
- That journey takes each one of us nearer and nearer to Christlikeness.

- Each of us, and our progress on our journey, is vitally important to God.
- The greater our likeness to Jesus, the more effectively God can do His work in the world through us.

People Builders

I began this chapter by saying that as we learn to love our brothers and sisters we discover that we are important. Our life begins to count. In Jesus, our life takes on real meaning and purpose for perhaps the first time.

What is it that gives us our significance? What is it that makes our life count?

No, it's not the roles we play in the institutional church. It's not our fame or success in society. Our significance is found in the fact that we can contribute to the one thing that will outlast the physical universe itself. *We can be used by God to build our brothers and sisters toward Christlikeness!* We can help them on their journey. By our love and caring, we can help our family grow in loyalty and in likeness to our Lord.

Whenever the Bible talks about "spiritual gifts" it is talking about the ministry of helping others grow. The Bible says several things very plainly about gifts.

Each of us has something to contribute. "To each one the manifestation of the spirit is given for the common good" (1 Cor. 12:7). To *each one.* This means that God has given *you* a special ability to contribute to others. Your contribution is needed for the common good. You can never say that you are insignificant or unimportant now, because God has given you a gift to share with others.

God Himself plans your contribution. "All these are the work of one and the same Spirit, and he gives them to each man, just as he determines" (1 Cor. 12:11). Because God is with you and works through you, you *can* make your contribution. Because God knows you intimately, He has fitted your personality and abilities with just the right contribution for you. You can never say that you are insignificant in the family of God, because God has chosen to work through you to build your brothers and sisters.

Our differences make us valuable. "God has arranged the parts in the body, every one of them, just as he wanted them to be" (1 Cor. 12:18). Picture a body. It has eyes, ears, a mouth, feet, hands—many many different parts. A body is so unique because each part is necessary to the well-being of the whole.

It's the same in the family of God. You are important *because you are different from others.* Thus what you have to contribute will be different. Just as a body would be a misshapen monstrous thing if it were all eye or all ear, so the family of God would be misshapen and monstrous if everyone were a preacher or a teacher. Instead God has planned our differences and arranged the way each of us fits into the family, so that all the needs of the Body of Christ will be met.

You can never say that you are unimportant in the family of God because God has given you a special place in His family, and what you have to contribute is necessary for the well-being of the whole.

As you contribute to your brothers and sisters in the family, you will grow together toward Christlikeness. "The whole body, joined and held together by every supporting ligament, grows and builds itself up in love, as each part does its work" (Eph. 4:16). As you do your part to build others and as they do their part in your life, you *will* grow together, "up into him who is the Head, that is, Christ" (4:15).

You can never again see yourself as unimportant. When God says *each part* has its work to do to build up others in love, realize that He is speaking about *you!*

What Contribution?

This talk of a "contribution to make" may be confusing—particularly if you're still thinking in institutional rather than family terms. Let me say it again. *People-building contributions are made as we build loving, brother-sister relationships with other Christians.*

Look, for instance, at some of the things the Bible lists as people-builders. Here are just a few. In Romans 12 we find serving, teaching, encouraging, contributing to others needs, leading, showing mercy. In 1 Corinthians 12 we find sharing a message of wisdom, faith, healing—even the gift of miracles is listed in that passage! But it's important to notice that wherever the Bible talks about making such contributions to others, it talks about building family relationships as the *context* for ministry!

Romans 12 directs us to "be devoted to each other in brotherly love. . . . Share with God's people in need. Practice hospitality. . . . Rejoice with those who rejoice; mourn with those who mourn. . . . Don't be proud, but be willing to associate with people of low position" (Rom. 12:10, 13, 15–16).

In Corinthians the Bible says that whatever we do without love will not count. It describes the relationships that build up others in this way: "Love is patient, love is kind. It does not envy, it does not boast, it is not proud. It is not rude, it is not self-seeking, it is not easily angered, it keeps no record of wrongs. Love . . . always protects, always trusts, always hopes, always perseveres" (1 Cor. 13:4–7).

Do you see it? When we come to know and love each other as family and build that brother–sister relationship that is ours in Christ, then we *will* come to know each other and share each other's life. As we share each other's life, there will be times when a word of encouragement or teaching, the sharing of wisdom, or even the sharing of material possessions, is just what our brother or sister needs to help him along his journey toward Christlikeness.

There will be times when a brother's faith wavers and we'll uphold him with our own trust in Jesus. Or times when our faith wavers and someone else ministers to us.

We'll live together as a family does, supporting each other in our commitment to Jesus, helping each other along the way.

This is why *you* are important: You are a member of the family of God. You belong with your brothers and sisters. And what you have to share with them is something they need to help them grow.

And you need them, too. We need each other to help each other become more and more like God.

Discovery 3

1. Think of a person who has helped you to grow as a person or as a Christian. Jot down a few words or phrases that describe this person. _____

_____

_____

_____

_____

2. In groups of four, share about the person you just described. Try to share in such a way that the others in your group will really come to know this person who has meant something to you and your growth. And listen closely as others share in turn.

3. Make a check mark on the continuum lines below to describe the person you just talked about.

a. As a person, he or she is

warm _____ cold

b. Our relationship was

close _____ distant

c. Our communication was

two way _____ one way

d. I felt that this person

cared _____ didn't care
for me   for me

e. I felt this person

knew me _____ didn't really
well   know me

4. Make a combined profile, discovering together the kind of person most likely to help others grow. What can you conclude about (1) the kind of person God uses and (2) the kind of relationship in which a supportive ministry takes place?

5. Work together through the "people builders" section of this chapter. Talk about what each of these "statements" has to say to you personally. (These statements also appear in the text in italics.)

a. Each of us has something to contribute. _____

_____

_____

b. God Himself plans your contribution. _____

_____

_____

c. Our differences make us valuable. _____

_____

_____

d. As you contribute, you will grow. _____

_____

_____

6. Seated in a circle, take just a moment to share with each of the others what in this session is or has been most meaningful to you personally.

4

OPEN WIDE THE DOORS

I suppose we have to admit it. Living in any family is a risky kind of thing. I mean, people who are that close to us come to know us too well. No one knows our weaknesses as well as the members of our family. Of course, no one better knows our strengths.

But it's the weaknesses that tend to frighten us. When we consider intimacy with other people, we realize that this means exposure of who we really are. And most of us aren't totally happy with who we are.

On a Journey

In the last chapter I suggested that we Christians are on a journey, a journey toward Christlikeness. We haven't arrived yet. But we're on the way. That's what Paul was saying in Corinthians when he assured us that we are "being transformed into his likeness with ever-increasing glory, which comes from the Lord, who is the Spirit" (2 Cor. 3:18). Our journey leads us onward toward the ever-increasing glory which is ours as we reflect Jesus more perfectly.

In the same Corinthians passage Paul deals with the hesitancy all of us feel when we think about risking intimacy—the risk of really becoming family and, in the intimacy of family, being known as we are. Paul begins by telling of an Old Testament event.

Moses had been called by God up to Mount Sinai to receive the stone tablets on which the Ten Commandments were written. When he came down from the mountain out of the presence of God, the Bible tells us that his face glowed with a brilliance so bright that "the Israelites could not look steadily" at him. But then Moses did a strange thing. He put a mask over his face (*see* Exod. 34:29–35).

The Old Testament doesn't explain this act, but Paul does in Corinthians. Paul says Moses put the mask on "to keep the Israelites from gazing at [his face] *while the radiance was fading away.*" There was a process of deterioration going on, and Moses did not want the Israelites to see the glory fade!

Paul applies this in a striking way. "We are very bold," he says of Christians. "We are not like Moses, who put a veil over his face." Instead Paul identifies us as those "who with unveiled faces all reflect the Lord's glory" (2 Cor. 3:12–13, 18).

Two things are vital here.

First, we are to live in the family with unveiled lives. This doesn't mean we immediately spill out all the hidden thoughts and feelings that trouble us the first time we meet another Christian. Not at all. It means gradually coming to know and love each other. It means realizing that as love relationships are established we can be ourselves in the family!

It means freedom from the awful loneliness of hiding all those unacceptable things about ourselves for fear that if others "really knew us" they would reject or despise us. It means realizing at last that we are loved by God and by others *in spite of* where we are on our journey, and it means discovering that we can share our real self in the family and still receive the support and the encouragement and the prayers we need to grow beyond whatever defeats us.

Second, even as imperfect persons we "all reflect the Lord's glory." This is very hard for us to grasp. How can human beings, who are *imperfect,* reflect God, who *is* perfect?

Paul's answer is unique. Others discover Jesus' glory in our lives *when they see us becoming* more like Him. It is the process of transformation itself that demonstrates the presence of Jesus. This is why Paul concludes his argument with that statement about transformation. We can reflect the Lord's glory, because we "are being transformed into his likeness with ever-increasing glory" (2 Cor. 3:18).

This is a very exciting truth. It means I don't have to wait until I'm perfect to glorify God. I don't have to wait until all my sins and weaknesses are overcome for God to work through me. I don't have to be *sinless* to be an effective Christian, and neither do you!

Instead, all we need to do is to open up our lives to God and to our brothers and sisters, and trust God to continue that transforming work in us—even though our weaknesses will be revealed (and this is why living with other Christians as family is a risk: our weaknesses *will* be revealed). God will gradually overcome them and change us. It is in the process of change that Jesus will be glorified.

A few years ago a young man was taken in by a Christian family. He had been a successful businessman, with a wife and two children. But his life had fallen apart as he turned to all sorts of sins. When our friends took him into their home upon his release from a local mental hospital, he was unable to speak in sentences. When anyone came to their home he would hide in a closet.

Two years later he was a different man. He had slowly come to trust Christ as he had been loved along by the larger family of Christians to which our friends belonged. His mind and his life were reconstructed, and his whole attitude changed.

I could never come into church and see him singing or hear him share a word in our congregational sharing time without being aware of the reality of Jesus Christ. Anyone who had known him *before,* now clearly saw the glory of God in his life.

Not everyone of us has that same kind of dramatic transformation. But each one of us who has a relationship with God through Jesus Christ *is* on a journey. Each one of us *is being transformed* by the Spirit of God at work in our lives, and everyone who is close enough to know us both *before* and *after* (that is, during the process) sees in our life the reflected glory of Jesus.

Close Enough

If we never get close enough for others to see our weaknesses, neither will they see the glorious process of God's transforming work in us. This is another reason why living together as family is so important. We are to live close enough to each other that we are known "before"—close enough so that masks can be taken off, and our true selves shared. We are to live close enough to each other that we can help each other with the process. (That's what that last chapter on "spiritual gifts" was all about.) We're to live close enough to each other so that we can rejoice together as we each take steps along the way of our journey toward Christlikeness—close enough to each other that we are known "after."

What does it take for us to open our lives to each other and become known?

1. *Assurance that we are loved—anyway.* God has made a great commitment to us. Now that we are His children, He *is for us.* He loves us so much that nothing in all creation can

separate us from His love. He loves us so much that He does not condemn. Instead, at our every failure He invites us to look to Jesus, standing before the throne of heaven to intercede for us. "Who is it that condemns?" the Bible asks. "Christ Jesus, who died—more than that, who was raised to life—is at the right hand of God and is also interceding for us" (Rom. 8:34).

God's love for us as His children is the model for the kind of love that we give each other. God is committed to us: His allegiance is unquestioned. He will be loyal to us through our failures and successes. We are to be just as loyal to our brothers and sisters, even through their failures and successes.

This context of allegiance—of loyalty to persons—is what we need in the family of God to free us to share our lives with one another. When I know that I am loved, anyway, I find the freedom to take off my mask and live with that unveiled face the Bible speaks about.

2. *Acceptance of our imperfections*. The Bible makes it painfully clear. In Christ I am a saint: but I am still a sinner. The potential for failure, for sin, remains with me. I still feel the tug of all the things I'd like to shake off. And sometimes I stumble. "I don't understand what I do," Paul complained in Romans 7. "For what I want to do I do not do, but what I hate I do" (Rom. 7:15).

It's not that I *have* to fail. Now that God is for me, I have the possibility of success! It's just that growth toward Christlikeness is a process; it's not an overnight kind of thing.

The small child learning to feed himself reaches out for the oatmeal but knocks over his milk. The eight year old, fearful of what Mommy will think, tells a sudden lie. At every stage of our growth as persons there are opportunities to succeed . . . and opportunities to fail.

Failing isn't all that serious. Really. The small child will learn to handle his glass of milk. The eight year old will learn to tell the truth. It's only when a failure becomes a fixed pattern of behavior that it's a serious problem. What we need to do with our failures is to admit them and try again until we succeed.

It's the same way with our life in Christ. Sometimes we'll do not what we want to do but what we hate and we won't understand later why we did it. At times like these it's good to know we can come to God and confess our sin and find full forgiveness—and be helped by God to grow beyond the failure to success.

But one thing is fatal: denying our failures. The Bible says, "if we claim to be without sin, we deceive ourselves and the truth is not in us. If we claim we have not sinned, we make him out to be a liar and his word has no place in our lives" (1 John 1:8, 10).

See what Scripture is saying? Don't deny that you have the potential to fail. After you have failed, don't pretend you didn't stumble. Be open and be honest.

If you don't feel the pressure to pretend with yourself, with God, or with other people, but realize that forgiveness is God's way of dealing with failure, it's much much easier to be open and real.

3. *Believe God is at work.* This is the third thing that helps us open up and develop intimacy in our Christian fellowship. The Bible says that "he who began a good work in you will carry it on to completion until the day of Christ Jesus" (Phil. 1:6).

You entered a relationship with God in Jesus Christ. God's commitment to you means that now He will work in your life to bring you to Christlikeness. It will take time. Sometimes we feel like only the barest beginning has been made. But God isn't discouraged. He "will carry it on to completion!"

It is this conviction that freed the apostle Paul to make that statement about unveiling in Corinthians. "We are being transformed," he shouts. "We are being transformed into His likeness." God is at work in us! And by His work we are assured of growth and change toward "ever-increasing glory."

If I am convinced that the direction of my life is toward godliness, and if I know that my brothers and sisters will rejoice with me as I find God at work in me, making me more and more like Him, it's so much easier for me to open up my life.

Thinking Back

What we've seen thus far is that each of us is on a journey toward Christlikeness. We share that journey with a family, and we open our lives to our brothers and sisters so they can rejoice with us as we grow.

Risking intimacy and opening our lives to others isn't easy. We're ashamed sometimes. We're afraid of what others will think. We wonder if we'll still be accepted. And then God comes with a word that brings us joy and freedom. *God tells us that our journey leads upward.* We are being *transformed!*

What's more, God will love us and support us along the way. He tells us that we can freely confess our sins and failures to Him, and He will be faithful and just to forgive our sins and cleanse us from all unrighteousness (*see* 1 John 1:9). He will be loyal to us all the way.

This is what Christian fellowship is to be. It is living together as a family of brothers and sisters who are loyal to each other, all the way. Loyal to each other, no matter what.

When I know that I have brothers and sisters in the family of God who love me and are loyal to me, then I can take the risk of being open with them. Then, as we open wide the doors of our lives to each other, we all see Jesus! We see Jesus, working lovingly in each other. We see Jesus, touching, transforming, progressively making us more like our Lord.

That's the promise that true Christian fellowship holds out for you—a family. A family of brothers and sisters who love you. A family who is loyal to you, all the way.

Well Worth the Risk

The Bible is a very exciting book. It doesn't just present ideas or concepts. It speaks the language of reality. What the Bible talks about is true, and because it is true we can experience it!

The Bible says that when we trust Christ as savior we enter a very special relationship with God. We can experience this relationship. The Bible also says that when we become one of God's children we become part of a family. And we can experience family relationships too!

Maybe you haven't ever been really close to other Christians. But you can be. It's possible you've never known others who are loyal to you, no matter what. But you can. It's even possible that you've never had the experience of loving other believers deeply, from the heart. But you can love them that way.

It's family that the Bible describes. And it's family that you and I are invited to experience. That's why even first steps toward fellowship are so important: just inviting some brothers or sisters over to your home, to share a meal, to visit, or play a game.

Perhaps best of all, a first step toward fellowship might be to form a small group with other Christians who also want to reach out with you, for a full experience of the wonderful promise of *family* that God has given to us as His people.

Discovery 4

1. Read 1 John 1:5–10. Before launching your study of 1 John, review together the content of chapter 4. Do this by first writing down below one concept from the chapter which seems to you to sum up its main teaching. _____

_____

_____

_____

_____

2. Share with one another what you have written. Then go on to look together at 1 John, which also deals with our failures and weaknesses.

3. What impact does hiding our sins or pretending we have no failings have on our relationship with God? Why (1 John 1:5–6)? _____

_____

_____

_____

4. How does *knowing* that we are loved and forgiven when we share a sin or weakness affect our freedom to be open and honest with God? How might it affect our freedom with others (1 John 1:9)? _____

_____

_____

_____

5. Why do we sometimes try to hide our failures from each other? Why is it important to learn to love, forgive, and accept each other in failures as well as triumphs (1 John 1:10)?

_____

_____

_____

_____

6. Do you know anyone who pretends and never admits faults? What is your opinion of him or her? Do you feel close to this person? Why, or why not? _____

_____

_____

_____

7. Which of the following two statements seems most important to you just now? Pick one, and then be prepared to share reasons for your choice with your study group.

    a. I can communicate God's love and forgiveness by not judging or condemning others for weaknesses they reveal.

    b. I can draw closer to others by being more open and refusing to hide my sins and weaknesses.

8. Share why you chose the statement you did.

5

NEED DOCTRINE DIVIDE?

In this book so far I've talked a lot about allegiance or loyalty. Now let's think together about another force that holds people together: conformity.

We can get at the notion of conformity by seeing the kinds of things that people have in common that lead them to form groups. Here are a few examples.

1. I want to go to the Arctic and explore. So I find others who share my passion for the cold. Because we have a common desire to explore in the Arctic, we form a group or team committed to that task.

2. I plan to go into the housing business. While I have some capital and some skills, there are other skills I lack, and more money is needed than I have. So I find others with the same desire who have the needed skills or cash, and we form a partnership.

3. I am very interested in drama and want to become an actor. I join a drama company in my home town and spend a lot of time with other aspiring actors. We raise money and put on plays locally and all hope for the big break that will take us to Broadway or Hollywood. In the meantime I polish my skills and enjoy the company of others who share my interest.

4. I am really into Eastern Religion. I've taken a class from the Maharishi Bashabashabashti and have my own mantras and everything. For awhile I hang around airports with others of the sect, wear a yellow robe (or, lately, a business suit), and try to sell slick books to travelers whom I never expect to see again.

Now, each of these illustrates a kind of association. In each a group has been formed, with a particular identity.

What does it take for a person to be accepted as part of one of these groups? How does a person continue to be a part of one?

First of all, for me to become a part of the group (whatever it is) there has to be some kind of decision on my part. I decide that my interest in the Arctic is strong enough to take steps to go there. Or I decide that I am willing to commit my money and my time to the housing business. Or I want to develop dramatically badly enough to join the drama group, learn my part in plays, and hang around with the others in the theater group. Or I decide to join the Maharishi's movement, and even put on those silly yellow robes and accost strangers.

I make a decision and act on it, and thus I become a group member.

But it takes more than my decision to become a part of these groups. I must have certain qualifications. I need to be physically able to brave the Arctic, for instance. (No explorers in their right minds would take along a ninety-year-old diabetic!) It's the same for the other groups. To become a part, I need qualifications: for the business partnership I need to have proven skills, or lots of money, or both. For the drama group I must have some level of talent. Even for the Maharishi I have to be courageous enough to harass travelers if I'm to fit in.

But there's more! Even if I get into the group, I must conform to retain my membership. If, at a meeting of Arctic

Explorers International, I suddenly say, "Hey, guys. Let's go to Hawaii instead," I won't be accepted for very long!

If I tell my business partners, "I want my money back," I'll no longer be a partner. If I stop coming to rehearsals or fail to turn up for the opening night, I'll soon be recognized as unreliable and unwanted! And as for the religious cult, well, unless I perform as expected, I will no longer be one of the disciples of the ol' Maharishi.

The point is simply this. *All human associations have certain requirements that must be met if a person is to get in— and stay in.* If we do not conform to the purposes or the practices of the group, we will not be allowed to belong.

This is only right. After all, how meaningful would it be to have an Arctic Explorers Club where everyone who joined wanted to go to the south seas? How viable would a business be if no one would commit money or time to it? To hold together, all human groupings *must have something in common,* and there are certain things members must conform to or they will be excluded from the group.

Excluded

Exclusion is, of course, the problem. Even when you get in, *you must conform to stay in.* You will not be accepted by the rest of the group unless you continue to see and do things the way they do.

In practice every group exerts many pressures to enforce conformity. Sometimes these pressures are in the form of rules which are clearly specified. "You must not miss more than two rehearsals." Other times the expectations are unstated, but nevertheless are real. If you violate an expectation, others won't talk to you. When you walk up to a small group there's an uneasy silence, and you know they've been talking about you, or about something that you can't be part of.

As far as all human institutions and organizations and even informal groups are concerned, the price of belonging is conformity. *If you do not conform, people will not let you belong.*

But let's go back to what the Bible says about Christianity. The reality of Christianity is that once we make our initial commitment to Jesus (and decide to join, as it were), God makes a permanent commitment to us. He takes us into His family. He calls us son or daughter. His commitment to us is forever. Nothing in the whole creation can separate us from the love of God in Christ Jesus our Lord.

So then God has made the announcement. You have trusted Christ? Then you are family. You do belong.

This reality must govern our attitude toward our brothers and sisters in Christ. *If God has accepted a person, then we cannot exclude him or her.* This is the real difference between the family of Christians and all other groups. Others may require conformity as the price of acceptance and belonging. Others can say we must have the same interests or live up to certain standards, or that we must agree with all the statements and interpretations of our leaders or the rule book. Others can say, "Conform, or you will not be allowed to belong."

But we Christians don't have that freedom! We can't say to a person whom God has accepted, "You don't belong, because you don't have the same list of don'ts that we have." You can't say to a brother, "There's no room for you in the family because your understanding of the Bible differs from mine."

God has called us together in a family, and He has told us to love each other, deeply. God has placed a priority on allegiance. God says we are to be loyal to one another. Because we are family, we cannot exclude others because they differ from us.

What About Doctrine?

Wars have been fought and great persecutions mounted because of differences in doctrine. Even today the church of Jesus Christ is tragically divided over honest differences in understanding of Scripture. More often than we might like to think, Christians exclude others from local fellowships because of differences in doctrine.

It would be unusual for you or I to be involved in the kind of dispute that rocks a denomination or that leads to the establishment of a new group. But there will be times when we're a part of a fellowship group with members who have very different beliefs than ours. What do we do then?

Because truth is important, are we duty bound to argue for our position and try to convert the others to our (correct) belief? Because truth is important, are we obligated to keep another person from sharing his or her "false doctrine," for fear that some might be led astray? Because truth is important, should we separate ourselves from others who have different views and form our own small branch of God's family on earth? And then keep our branch "pure" by insisting that only those who believe as we do can belong?

In 1 Corinthians the Bible records a fascinating test case showing us how to deal with doctrinal disagreement. The believers at Corinth were divided about eating food that had been sacrificed to idols. This was not a difference over convictions. This was a debate about doctrine. Some said, "That's taking part in demon worship!" Others said, "An idol is just a piece of wood or hunk of metal: only God is real."

Now, that's an important doctrinal question. Are idols and idol worship nothing? Or were demons behind the pagan worship of the non-Christians of Corinth?

As with all doctrinal disputes, the consequences in Corinth were disturbing. Those who believed idols were nothing would drop into the temple meat market and pick up a steak or roast cut from a sacrificial animal sold by the priests to help support the pagan temple. Those who believed that demons were behind pagan worship were convinced that eating such meat was participating in rites related to demonism. A very serious division grew up between the two groups. It's no wonder that one faction had a hard time accepting the other! It's no wonder that those who were convinced that their brothers and sisters were getting involved with demons pressured them to stop eating such meat.

How did God's family in Corinth resolve the dispute? Did one faction surrender its view of truth? Or did they decide to set up rival congregations [the Methodist Meat-Eaters vs. the Methodist Never-From-a-Pagan-Sacrifice-Eaters]? Or they simply decided not to speak to each other? Or one faction simply gave in, and surrendered its distinctive point of view?

This is how the apostle Paul dealt with the question. He wrote in 1 Corinthians 8:1–3, "Now about food sacrificed to idols: We know that we all possess knowledge. Knowledge puffs up, but love builds up. The man who thinks he knows something does not yet know as he ought to know. But the man who loves God is known by God" (or, as PHILLIPS puts it, "is opening up his whole life to the Spirit of God"). Let's look at what he was saying point by point.

We all do have knowledge. That is, each side based its position on its grasp of truth as God has revealed truth in the Scriptures and the apostles' teachings. So both argue from their understanding of truth.

That knowledge is imperfect. This is what Paul meant when he wrote "the man who thinks he knows something does not yet know as he ought to know." We all have some grasp of God's truth because He has revealed it. But we do not know the *whole truth!* We must always preface our statements about doctrine with, "As I understand it . . . ." or "As I believe the Bible teaches. . . ."

This doesn't mean that the Bible isn't clear, or that there hasn't been general agreement among Christians throughout history about its basic teachings. There is that kind of agreement. But it does mean that every human being is fallible. We can be mistaken. No matter how well we do understand, we do not yet know as perfectly as God.

Do you see the importance of this teaching? It means that we must hold our doctrines *humbly*. It means that we can never say to a brother "You *must* believe as I do because *I have the truth!*" We must be humble and open to gain a greater understanding of truth than we now have. If I hold my doctrines humbly, I must give my brother freedom to disagree with me—even if what we disagree about is important.

Knowledge inspires pride. This is part of the warning Paul gave when he said "knowledge puffs up." If I am sure that *I am right* then I am equally sure that my brother is wrong. However graciously I may want to put it, this means that I *see myself as superior* to him.

The spiritual pride expressed by insisting that our doctrines are right and are in fact the only right way to see the issue is totally destructive to Christian fellowship. The Bible says, "in humility consider others better than yourselves" (Phil. 2:3). We must guard against any attitude of spiritual pride that will keep us from loving our brothers and sisters and honoring them.

We can, and should, seek to discover God's truth and to understand it. Of course we want to be convinced of our doctrinal positions. But we can never let our knowledge convince us that we know the whole truth or allow us to reject a brother or sister because his or her understanding is different from ours.

Love is a better approach. This is the way that Paul pointed to when he contrasted love with knowledge and said, "love builds up."

Love puts the priority on persons. Love says, "I have an unshakeable allegiance to you, in spite of our differences."

And note the significance of the term "builds up." "Upbuilding" is intimately related to the journey toward transformation that all of God's children are taking. In fact it is as we minister to and support each other that "the whole body, joined and held together by every supporting ligament, grows and builds itself up in love, as each part does its work" (Eph. 4:16).

We are to stay linked together. We are to love each other. We are each to use our gifts to build into the lives of others in the family. And as we do, we grow up into Jesus Christ.

Time Is Important

As soon as we see the issue in terms of growth everything falls into place. *We can expect all of God's children— ourselves included—to grow and to change.* What we need to do is to affirm our allegiance to brothers and sisters who differ from us, and give them—and us—time to grow!

This is why love is so important. Love creates the context for growth. In the family, where I know I am accepted, I have the opportunity to be my real self. As I open up my life to others I am also opening up myself to God. It is through love that we as a whole family mature and are built up in our faith.

Think about it for a moment: If I fight my brother, I make him defend his ideas. If I fight my brother, I make him defend himself against me. If I fight my brother, then one of us must lose and one must win when our differences are resolved. No one likes to lose; so if I fight my brother, he will close his mind and heart to what I have to say and struggle to maintain his own beliefs against me.

And think about this: If I love my brother, he can share his ideas without feeling he has to defend them. If I love my brother, he never feels that I am a danger to him, even though

I may disagree. If I love my brother, when we finally come to a common understanding of God's truth, then we both will have won. If I love my brother, he can open his heart and mind to what I have to say without having to struggle against me.

In Corinthians Paul did go on to explain which point of view about idols and demons was right. He didn't hesitate to speak the truth. But he spent most of his time in the passage (1 Cor. 8–10) showing the brothers how to relate to each other in love. And he helped them not to ask, "Am I right?" but to ask instead, "Am I showing love to my brother?"

This is another very exciting thing about being in the family of God: We don't have to demand conformity—even doctrinal conformity—as a condition for acceptance and love. If you are a child of God and profess faith in Jesus Christ, then I affirm you as my brother or sister. I will love you and be loyal to you even when we disagree.

One more thing. What if some who claim to be Christians really aren't? Can they be identified by false doctrine? Should they be thrust out of the family then?

Well, yes . . . and no. No, in that we aren't to be quick in judging if another person is a true believer or not. Some folks simply take a lot of loving to grow in their understanding of God's truth. God really did not give you or me the right to examine others and say to some, "You're in," and to others, "You're out!" If people profess Christ, then we are to accept and love them until they prove themselves not to be believers.

How do people do that? John answered this question beautifully. "They went out from us, but they did not really belong to us. For if they had belonged to us, they would have remained with us; but their going showed that none of them belonged to us" (1 John 2:19).

The people who are not really believers (John's word is stronger than that: antichrist) simply will not stay in the family. We don't put them out. They choose to leave.

That's another fascinating thing about love. For those of us who are God's children, family love draws us in, enriches our lives, and helps us to grow. For those who are not God's children, family love is so painful that ultimately they leave us.

So you see, there's no real risk in loving a brother or sister who differs doctrinally. Even on something important. If they're in the family, our love will help them (and us) grow to a better understanding of God's truth.

If the people I reach out to love aren't brothers or sisters, in time those people will leave by their own choice. And the church of Jesus Christ will both be loving and doctrinally pure.

Discovery 5

1. Read 1 John 2:3–11. Before launching your study of 1 John, review together the content of chapter 5. Do this by first writing down one concept from the chapter which seems to you to sum up its main teaching. Write here: _____

_____

_____

_____

2. Share with one another what you have written. Then go on to look at 1 John, which also deals with the basis of relationships.

3. How do we know we are in fellowship with God even if we may not feel close to Him at times (1 John 2:3)? _____

_____

_____

_____

4. What is the difference between a "doctrinal" test of fellowship and the test of fellowship identified in 1 John 2:4?

_____

_____

5. What will be the outcome of obedience as far as relationships within God's family are concerned? How is this related to walking "as Jesus did" (1 John 2:5–6)?

_____

_____

6. What is the implication if we reject, draw back from, or refuse to accept a person who is a brother or sister (1 John 2:9–11)? _____

7. How does this passage in John relate to the content of the chapter? _____

_____

_____

_____

8. How does this passage in John relate to my own life and personal relationships now? _____

_____

_____

_____

_____

_____

6

LOOK UP, NOT DOWN!

One of the most common threats to allegiance in the family is what we call "convictions." All too often brothers and sisters are made to feel that they aren't acceptable because of some practice they engage in that others in the group do not.

I remember unexpectedly meeting on the streets of Brooklyn one day a man who sang beside me in the choir of our Baptist church. Although he was a detective in the New York city police force, he looked like an embarrassed child as he tried to hide a lit cigarette in one cupped hand as he talked with me and some of the other young people. You see, in that church we had convictions against cigarettes. Our brother was afraid he wouldn't be accepted or loved if we knew he smoked.

Before you start feeling that I'm rather down on Baptists, let me clear that up. Our little church in Bay Ridge was God's gift to me, just when I needed fellowship most. I did many foolish things there and I was loved anyway. None of us in that church was perfect. Some of the things that the congregation held most dear I now believe were wrong. But they were my family and I loved them, and they loved me. I still love them.

They do not have to be right or be perfect to be family.

So I'm not at all negative about my days in that congregation. It was there that I first learned by experience something of what it means to be in the family of God. Still, we *weren't* perfect, and sometimes we let our convictions become barriers between us and other brothers and sisters in God's family. Sometimes we were loyal to our convictions—but not loyal to God's people.

Convictions

What are convictions? Usually they're not doctrines as such. Instead they are practices that we justify on the basis of reasoning from Scripture. Doctrine focuses on what we believe. Convictions focus on what we do.

We can find many illustrations of convictions. Here are just a few of the practices that are important to some people and have become tests of acceptance into Christian fellowships. For instance:

> smoking
> drinking alcoholic beverages
> allowing teens to dance
> using certain musical instruments in church
> going to movies
> wearing makeup
> always having church service at 11 o'clock on
> Sunday mornings
> buying or selling on Sundays

We could go on and add other things to this list, but this gives us a clear idea of what convictions are.

It's not wrong for an individual to have convictions. In fact, it's a good thing to examine our lifestyle and our practices, and to determine which things might be displeasing to the Lord. But we get into trouble when we insist that *our* convictions are normative for other Christians. It's when we insist that the convictions we hold must govern the lives of others that we have a family problem.

Looking Back

It's helpful to recall the assumptions underlying our thinking about Christian fellowship. The basics are these:

- In Christ, individuals enter into a special Father/child relationship with God. They become part of His family.

- The fact that in Christ we are family is an unchangeable reality. All of God's children become my brothers and my sisters.

- It follows that "belonging" for Christians is based on personal relationship with God. If God has accepted an individual in Christ then, no matter what, that person is my brother or sister. I'm not really free to set up conditions under which I'll accept a person who belongs to Christ. If God has accepted her or him, then I must acknowledge that person as a brother or sister and love him as family.

- It is allegiance to persons then, rather than conformity to distinctives and differences between Christians, that is the key to Christian fellowship. We are called to be loyal to the family , to love the family, in spite of any differences.

These are the very principles Paul applied in his instruction to the Corinthians about division over doctrinal issues. He told them to admit that their knowledge was incomplete. He showed them that to try to base fellowship on doctrinal agreement is dangerous. It puffs up and divides. Instead, they were to rely on love. Love builds up. As we love each other, we all will grow, and growth will lead us to a more perfect understanding as well as to Christlikeness.

Paul did go on to correct their misunderstanding of the doctrine involved. He didn't suggest that doctrine was unimportant. He made a simple appeal for love and acceptance and loyalty to continue . . . and for each one to give the others plenty of time.

Yet when it came to differences over convictions, Paul was very blunt. He tells us unequivocally, as he told the Corinthians, to let others hold their convictions while we hold ours. We are never to impose convictions on our brothers or sisters!

The Vegetarian Connection

Eating only vegetables was one conviction that divided the church in Rome. Some said Christians ought not to eat any meat. Others said, in effect, "That's ridiculous!"

That conflict and another are discussed in Romans 14. The other difference was over holy days. Is Sunday "special?" Or is every day a holy day? In the Rome of Paul's day, differences over both of these Christian practices stirred up strong emotions. People on both sides held their own convictions dearly.

There were two particular results of conflict over convictions that struck at the unity of the family: (1) looking down on others and (2) condemning others. This threat to allegiance is what Paul dealt with immediately. "The man who eats everything must not look down on him who does not, and the man who does not eat everything must not condemn the man who does" (Rom. 14:3). Paul understood very clearly just how we react when someone's convictions differ from ours.

"What! You don't wear makeup! Why, isn't that silly. Mabel, did you know Helen here won't wear makeup because she thinks it's not Christian?"

When we look down on a brother or sister, or put them down like this, we are violating the principle of allegiance. We are not *loving*—love involves respect as well as affection. Remember that phrase from Philippians where Paul warns us against "vain conceit" and goes on to say that "in humility consider others better than yourselves?" (Phil. 2:3). Well, *that* is loving. Looking down on a brother or sister for his or her convictions is not.

The other reaction is just as bad. "Did you see that Mabel? Why, she even wore a dab of lipstick to *church!* Looked just like a harlot, she did, all painted up like that."

That is "condemning," and God says, we "must not condemn the man who does, for God has accepted him. Who are you to judge someone else's servant? To his own master he stands or falls. And he will stand, for God is able to make him stand" (Rom. 14:3–4).

Put simply, Paul was saying this: Jesus is Lord. Not you, and not me. Christians give an account to God for their convictions, *not* to other Christians. We are accountable to our Master. God has not made us slaves to other men.

Lordship Is the Issue

It is really hard for us to grasp, but when it comes to convictions, people on opposite sides of an issue can *both* be right!

Let's go back to the issues concerning the Romans. Paul said, "One man considers one day more sacred than another; another man considers every day alike. Each one should be fully convinced in his own mind. He who regards one day as special does so to the Lord. He who eats meat, eats to the Lord, for he gives thanks to God; and he who abstains, does so to the Lord and gives thanks to God" (Rom. 14:5–6).

It is not *what* we do that is "right." It is the fact that we are convinced in our own minds that this is the way we can best honor God. It is that we do what we do "as to the Lord."

See how terrible it would be if I were to use pressure to make others conform to my convictions? See how wrong it would be if, as a member of a group of Christians, I insisted that, to be accepted and to belong, others would have to conform their practices to ours?

Paul said in Romans, "For this very reason, Christ died and returned to life so that he might be the Lord of both the dead and the living. You, then, why do you judge your brother? Or why do you look down on your brother?" (14:9–10).

Do you see it? *Jesus is Lord*. And each of us is to be directly responsible to Him.

If I am to help my brother grow in responsiveness to the Lord, then I must do nothing that pressures him to conform to my views and my convictions, as if I were God to him. Because Jesus is Lord, I can neither look down on my brother nor judge him. In the family we cannot set up any such practices as a condition of fellowship.

I am to love my brothers and sisters—not judge them.

I am to love my brothers and sisters—not look down on them

I am to love my brothers and sisters—and let Jesus be their only Lord.

Love in Action

In this fascinating story in the book of Romans, Paul guides us to look away from the "thing itself" about which we have convictions. We are not to argue about whether all those things I listed earlier are right or wrong. We can of course share our own convictions about them. But we must also give others freedom to develop their own convictions and neither condemn them nor look down on them, whatever they decide.

But extending this kind of freedom to others does not mean we demand it for ourselves! This is the other side of love in action.

In this same passage Paul talked about "weaker" and "stronger" brothers. What characterizes each? Well, the "weak" brother is the one who says "I can't" when it comes to eating meat. He is the one who fails to grasp the freedom that we have in Christ, and finds the action wrong in itself. It is the stronger brother who has come to realize that "there is no food unclean in itself" (Rom. 14:14). In essence, the people with the "really strong convictions" are the weak Christians!

But how do the "strong," who have a clearer focus on what is important to God, relate to the weak? Because we have freedom, do we demand the right to exercise it? Because we do not judge or look down on our brothers, do we insist that they stop judging us?

In Paul's fascinating answer to this question, he once again focused on loyalty to our brothers and sisters. "Do not by your eating destroy your brother for whom Christ died" (Rom. 14:15). Paul said very plainly that "if your brother is distressed because of what you eat, you are no longer acting in love" (14:15). We are to consider the convictions of our brothers and sisters when we choose what we will do with our freedom.

Paul was warning us against parading our freedom— flaunting our ability to do in good conscience what someone else in good conscience cannot do. Flaunting freedom simply isn't love.

When the Bible argues that the "thing itself" is not unclean, God also is saying that things are *unimportant*. I may have a right to my steak dinner. But whether I eat steak or not doesn't really matter. I may have freedom to take a social drink. But whether I sip that cocktail or refuse it doesn't really matter. I may use instruments in my church services, but whether I do or not really isn't the issue.

What *is* the issue? "The kingdom of God is not a matter of eating and drinking, but of righteousness, peace and joy in the Holy Spirit, because anyone who serves Christ in this way is pleasing to God and approved by men" (Rom. 14:17–18). What matters is this question: "What is God's kingdom all about?" God's kingdom isn't built on what we eat or don't eat. God's kingdom is brought to present reality as the family of God lives together in righteousness, peace, and joy.

What is important is living together in love, so that we can go on growing together in righteousness—growing together in peace to be an even more closely knit and loving family—growing in joy, a joy which is not spoiled by looking down on our brothers or by judging them.

So Look Up, Not Down

God's message to us on this issue of convictions is to look up, not down. Look up and let Jesus be Lord in your own life. And in the life of others.

Stop judging the brother who "does." Stop looking down on the brother who "can't." Affirm with God what is really important—that we live together in love, in spite of differences we may have. Unshaken, we hold our allegiance to those in the family of God whose convictions are different from our own.

Discovery 6

1. Read 1 John 2:15–17. Before your study of 1 John, review together the content of chapter 6. Do this by first writing down one concept from the chapter that seems to you to sum up its main teaching. Write here: _____

_____

_____

_____

_____

2. Share with one another what you have written. Then go on to look at the 1 John passage, which also deals with what we call "worldliness."

3. Think of one thing you wanted badly as a child or adult. Write it down here: _____

_____

4. In groups of four, share together about the thing you wrote down:

    a. Why did you want it? b. What happened to it? c. Did getting it satisfy you, or did not getting it destroy you?

5. John has three things which he says identifies "everything in the world." What do each of these represent to you?

    a. cravings
    b. lust of the eyes
    c. boasting (pride) of what he has and does

6. How does 1 John 2 relate to Paul's teaching that the "thing itself" is not wrong or "worldly"?

7. From this chapter's study and 1 John 2, what is the one most significant thing you have learned personally, and how do you intend to apply it to your life? _____

_____

_____

_____

7

WHAT ABOUT DISCIPLINE?

Carla was in one of the small fellowship groups I participated in in Phoenix. She'd been brought up to feel bad about herself and had a hard time loving or being loved. She often spoke bitterly about experiences in her home church, where conformity was required and she never felt accepted. But Carla seemed to be making progress.

Then she took a job as organist at a church in the community. There she met a leader of that congregation. She began dating him, even though he was married. Before long they were having an affair.

Carla stopped coming regularly to our fellowship group, but she did spend a lot of time with the two newest Christians in our group. She told them daily what was happening in her relationship and she also argued vehemently that what she was doing was right.

Even when the man left his wife and two children to live with her, she tried to argue from the Bible ("the Greek says" was her favorite phrase) that their relationship was not sin.

One evening as our group met, one of the women shared the situation and her own feelings. She was deeply troubled.

She knew that what Carla was doing was wrong. And she felt that Carla was using her, trying to justify her actions with excuses she'd given to herself. She did love Carla and wanted Carla to know it. But she wasn't sure *how* to love Carla in this situation. Certainly she wasn't helping Carla any now.

How to Love

How to express love is one of our greatest problems as Christians. We're a family now. We want the best for our brothers and sisters. But often we don't understand how to love them wisely.

I can understand those who are so committed to God's Word as they understand it that they want to share its marvelous truths with others. I can understand how upset they become when another person can't seem to see or accept a doctrine that is vital or especially meaningful. I understand because I feel the same way myself. But I've learned that confronting others about doctrine or demanding that they believe as I do as the price of admission to fellowship isn't God's way. And it is not loving.

"The Lord's servant must not quarrel," Paul said to Timothy; "instead he must be kind to everyone, able to teach, not resentful. Those who oppose him he must gently instruct, in the hope that God will grant them repentance leading them to a knowledge of the truth" (2 Tim. 2:24–25). Love, the way of kindness and gentleness, does not permit us to quarrel over doctrine. We're to keep on loving and keep on being loyal to our brother or sister, even when we differ.

I can understand how those with strong convictions are troubled when other Christians don't see issues the same way they do. After all, we're to arrive at our convictions by being "fully persuaded in our own minds" that what we do pleases God. After I've been through that process of persuading myself about my convictions, it's very difficult to see a brother or sister come up with a conclusion opposite to my own!

But God's Word is very clear here. Even where there are significant differences, I am to let Jesus be Lord in my brother's life. I give my brother freedom to hold his own convictions, and I must not *condemn him* for them or *look down on him* for them. Instead I am simply to keep on loving him. I am to be loyal in my allegiance to him as a fellow member of God's family.

But somehow that situation with Carla seems different. It wasn't a matter of conviction, but of open sin. Does the restriction on judging operate here too? Is it loving for me to let my sister hug her sin to her without a word? I know I must keep on loving her and be loyal. But how?

Judging

To see how the Bible deals with sin in the family, we need more insight into "judging." We have seen Paul state flatly, "Who are you to judge another man's servant!" In this he seems to cut us off from using our critical faculties to evaluate others.

But this isn't the case at all! To see why, we need to examine *what* is being judged in several New Testament passages about judging.

Romans 14. We have already explored this passage. We know that here Paul has written about judging another person's convictions. This, Scripture says, we have no right to do. We can each judge what we ourselves are to do to please God in areas of conviction. But we are not to judge others.

Please note this. In an area of "convictions" there is no specific biblical "thou shalt" or "thou shalt not." That's why we have such great differences over convictions. We reason out our convictions in the light of Scripture and our culture. But we can't say, "Here is what the Lord says," in matters of personal conviction.

No wonder James insisted we are not to slander one another or speak against our brothers. To do such things puts us in the place of God who is judge and lawgiver. Our obligation is simply to do God's will as well as we can (*see* James 5:11–12).

Matthew 7:1–5. "Do not judge, or you too will be judged. . . . Why do you look at the speck of sawdust in your brother's eye and pay no attention to the plank in your own eye?" With these and other exhortations, Jesus helps us see that we are not appointed to examine or pass judgment on the attitudes or actions of other Christians, but instead we are to examine our own. Our brother's behavior is not subject to our judgment, nor are his motives.

This last point is very important. Paul said, "who among men knows the thoughts of a man except the man's spirit within him?" (1 Cor. 2:11). Motives are hidden from us. Yet God cares deeply about motives. For example, in Romans 14 it was the motive for eating or not eating meat that was the critical issue. Either conviction could be held "to the Lord" and be honoring to Him. As long as we don't know the heart of our brothers or sisters—and we can't really know their heart—we have no way to judge their attitudes or actions.

1 Corinthians 6:1–6. "If any of you has a dispute with another, dare he take it before the ungodly for judgment instead of before the saints? . . . Are you not competent to judge trivial cases?"

Now suddenly we read what seems to be just the opposite! Here we are told that Christians *are* to judge!

How do we reconcile the apparent contradiction? "Don't judge," says Romans 14. "Don't judge," says James 5. "Don't judge," says Matthew 7. Yet "Do judge," says 1 Corinthians 6!

But look at *what* is to be judged.

Don't judge . . . another's actions that express his or her personal convictions.

Don't judge . . . another's behavior that expresses his or her efforts to live by God's Word.

Don't judge . . . the motives or thoughts of a brother or sister's heart.

But *do* step in and help settle a dispute in the family that might otherwise take believers to the courts. Become involved and help family members determine the fair thing to do.

1 Corinthians 5:1–13. At this point we can better understand why Paul wrote concerning another situation, "I have already passed judgment on the one who did this, just as if I were present" (5:3). Paul would never have passed judgment on others for their convictions. He would never have judged their motives. But here he was dealing with a different issue.

In fact, he was dealing with a situation just like Carla's, in which a brother had moved into a relationship that involved the consistent practice of what Scripture identifies as sin. When it comes to clear and unmistakable and consistent practice of sin, *then* the family *is* to judge.

"It's actually reported that there is sexual immorality among you." Paul wrote in a shocked tone. "And you are proud! Shouldn't you rather have been filled with grief and have put out of your fellowship the man who did this?" Paul went on to give explicit instructions. "I am writing you that you must not associate with anyone who calls himself a brother but is sexually immoral or greedy, an idolator or a slanderer, a drunkard or a swindler. With such a man do not even eat!" For, he wrote, *"Are you not to judge those inside?"*

Please note. Motives are not being judged here. Convictions are not being judged here. What is being judged are actions which the Bible reveals unmistakably to be sin.

In a way, even this isn't "judging." It's agreeing with God's judgment. You see, we aren't the ones who say on our own authority that sexual immorality and swindling are wrong. It is

God who has made that determination. Since we, as God's children, have given Him our full allegiance, we *agree with His judgment*. Our allegiance to God means that we must react to sin as He does.

The Loving Thing to Do

There are several things to notice in this passage. First, we are to agree with God's judgment that certain things revealed to us as sin *are* sin.

Second, it's not the occasional failure that calls for discipline. The words Paul used here do not describe a single slip, but a pattern of life. A brother who is "sexually immoral" has chosen an immoral way of life. An "idolator" keeps on practicing idol worship. A "slanderer" makes character assassination a regular practice. A "swindler" earns his living (or a good part of it) dishonestly. A "drunkard" isn't the person who has an occasional cocktail, but one for whom alcoholism is a way of life.

Third, we are to *exclude from fellowship* a person who "calls himself a brother" but makes a habit of such practices. Paul said, "don't even eat with such a man" (1 Cor. 5:11) and "expel the wicked man from among you" (1 Cor. 5:13).

At first this seems to go against everything we've seen in Scripture about loyalty to brothers and sisters. How can we maintain the family relationship and the allegiance it demands by excluding? How is it loving to cut a person off from our fellowship?

The goal is both protection and restoration. The rest of the family is to be protected from contamination by sin. "Don't you know that a little yeast works its way through the whole batch of dough?" Paul asked. "Get rid of the old yeast that you may be a new batch without yeast" (1 Cor. 5:6–7). We are to be a family that carries the likeness of Jesus, and He is not a practicer of sin.

But how about the individual who's excluded? In Paul's second letter to the Corinthians we see the outcome of the immorality incident. The Corinthian family had excluded the sinning brother from fellowship, and as a result this brother stopped his practice of sin! So Paul wrote, "the punishment inflicted on him by the majority is sufficient for him. Now instead you ought to forgive and comfort him, so that he will not be overwhelmed by excessive sorrow. I urge you therefore, to reaffirm your love to him" (2 Cor. 2:6–7). Discipline by the family restored the straying brother to fellowship.

Discipline is to reproduce on earth the reality of what has happened in heaven. The Bible is clear about the impact of the practice of sin on our relationship with God. "Your iniquities have separated you from your God," the Old Testament prophet announced (Isa. 59:2). The Bible says very clearly that "if we claim to have fellowship with him yet walk in the darkness, we lie and do not live by the truth" (1 John 1:6). The habitual practice of sin cuts us off from fellowship with God.

Remember Carla? Remember how she argued that she was *not* sinning? She had deceived herself about her present relationship with God. She claimed to have fellowship with Him, in spite of the fact that she was walking in darkness. She was lying—to others, but also to herself.

How *can* God communicate with a person who will not listen to Him? God's answer is to have the family on earth *act out the reality of the break in fellowship with God!* Carla might deceive herself about how God sees her actions. But Carla can't pretend everything is all right if God's people— her family and His—cut her off from fellowship. She can't pretend that her actions are acceptable when the family will not accept them!

This is what discipline is all about. We agree with God in His judgment of sin. We keep everyone clear on the fact that God's family is called to be Christlike and thus will not make sin a practice. We help a brother or sister who has turned aside realize how serious a sinful way of life is to help him return to God and get on with his journey toward Christlikeness.

The Power of Love

Actually, the effectiveness of "church discipline" in motivating a return to God is related directly to the level of love within the family. If I know and love my brothers and sisters, and if I know they care for me, then discipline will hurt. If love has given me a deep sense of belonging, then my exclusion will touch me deeply.

On the other hand, if my relationships with Christians are superficial, I won't mind if people at the church I attend exclude me. I'll just pack up and find another church where my secret isn't known and I can go on pretending that everything is all right.

How great the power of love is! Where I am truly and deeply loved, and where I love in return, all pretense is stripped away. There, in the family, I have that deep sense of joy and belonging. The power of that deep and real family love will support me and help me turn away from sin—even when something inside pulls me toward it.

But heed this one warning. Withdrawal of fellowship by the family is to be used *only* in the case of consistent practice of sin.

Not for doctrinal differences, not for divergence in convictions, not as a tool for leaders to manipulate members of the local family or to force compliance. Withdrawal of fellowship is never to be used over any issue except one that God Himself has clearly defined in Scripture to be sin.

Love is too powerful to be misused. Love is too wonderful to be perverted. Love is too great a gift to be used to any ungodly end.

Discovery 7

1. Read 1 John 2:18–27. Before your study of 1 John, review together the content of chapter 7. Do so by completing each of the following sentences.

    a. Three things I am not called by God to judge are:

       1) _____

       2) _____

       3) _____

    b. As a Christian I am called by God to judge (believers/unbelievers) when their actions _____

       _____

2. The purpose of "discipline" in the church is:

    a. _____

    b. _____

3. Love is expressed in church discipline by _____

_____

_____

_____

4. First John 2:18–19 speaks of "anti" (against) Christs. How are they removed from fellowship? How are they *not* removed? _____

_____

_____

_____

_____

5. God's Spirit helps those who are His come to know the truth. How can realizing this truth free us from fear of others and from defensiveness? What is important here for fellowship (1 John 2:20–23)? _____

_____

_____

_____

6. Do we need to fear those who through ignorance or in an attempt to be devisive try to teach false doctrines? Why, or why not (1 John 2:24–27)? _____

_____

_____

_____

7. Which of the following statements seem to be true? How might you change any you disagree with to better express the concepts taught in this chapter and 1 John 2:18–27?

   a. Christians are to watch for every slip by other believers and correct or discipline them firmly.
   b. We are to discipline others for habitual sin and for doctrinal deviation.
   c. As we love and share with others who differ from us they will choose to leave by themselves, if they are not of God's family.
   d. God did not make you or I responsible to determine who is and who is not a "true Christian."

8

VERY PERSONAL BIBLE STUDY

One of the most enjoyable aspects of family life comes when we gather as brothers and sisters to explore God's Word. The family comes together to listen to the Father and to tell Him how much we appreciate Him.

New Life

When we become Christians God has, in Paul's words, "rescued us from the dominion of darkness and brought us into the kingdom of the Son he loves" (Col. 1:13). We're taken out of the old world we once lived in and placed in a new world. Our old relationships, attitudes, values, ways of thinking and living—all these are now gradually being replaced as we journey toward Christlikeness.

But how are we to discover what Christ is like? How do we learn His values? How do we come to see life from His perspective? We find an answer when we remember that in the Bible we have the very thoughts of God and that God will give me new understanding as we explore His thoughts.

But there's another important purpose in Bible study. The

Bible is a living Word. In Scripture we not only have a record of what God has said. We also have a vibrant gift which the Holy Spirit uses to give personal guidance, now.

Recently I went through a time of great tension and strain. Almost daily the Holy Spirit lifted out of the Scripture I was reading some thought or phrase to impress on my mind. There were words of comfort when I needed encouragement. There was correction when I needed restraint. There were promises when I needed hope, and guidance when I was uncertain. God spoke in unmistakable ways, and His living voice both met my needs and graciously shaped me into a likeness more like Christ's.

Looking at the Bible, then, I realize it is a deeply personal book. It is God's Word for me. It is God's voice to me. I study Scripture both to understand God and to meet Him.

I use different approaches to study the Bible for under-standing and for a personal meeting with God. To learn God's viewpoint and grasp His way of thinking, I use a method we can call "tracing the Bible's developed thought."

The Bible wasn't given to us in random fragments. In most cases it comprises carefully reasoned letters or purposefully described sequences of events. So before I hastily interpret or apply a verse, I need to see how it fits into the flow of thought (or context) of the passage. Often seeing a verse in the context of the larger thought unit gives me a completely new insight into its meaning.

I've found that a good way to do this kind of Bible study is to use a version that divides the text into paragraphs (like the NIV or RSV). I try to summarize each entire paragraph in a single sentence. This doesn't mean using words from the text over and over again, but trying to capture the thought in my own words. Then I move on to the next paragraph and so work through the whole thought unit. Then I blend the sentences together into a summary paragraph. Finally, I can go back and look through the text guided by this "thought outline" of the whole passage.

For example, here's a passage that talks about unity in the church family: 1 Corinthians 1–4. Four whole chapters are summarized to capture the main issues—ideas we'll explore more in our chapter on leadership in God's family.

1 Corinthians 1–4

I urge you to resolve your differences and restore unity in the church family. Remember, Christ is the center of our life and in Him we *are* one.

This may not sound like a very "wise" argument, but then the message of Christ and His cross has always been at odds with human wisdom. And Christ, not some super "wisdom," brought you your righteousness, holiness, and redemption. That's why I kept my message simple when I was with you. I wanted you to rely only on the crucified Lord.

Of course, there is a divine wisdom. But it comes by revelation, and not human discovery. This wisdom involves learning to think God's thoughts, something that requires both hearing the revealed words and being enlightened by the Holy Spirit.

But you! Why, your jealousy and quarreling make it very clear that you think and act like mere men. Who do you think is important: we servants or God who works through us? I'm thankful that I can serve, but my foundation is Jesus, and one day what I build will be evaluated. (Don't you even grasp the fact that the true construction is going on *in your lives;* that *you* are God's sacred temple? Building up people, not tearing them down, is doing God's work!)

So don't deceive yourselves with all those childish arguments over leaders. Abandon that foolish game and focus again on all that is yours in Jesus. Can't you grasp the basic principle? God Himself is the source of all. How then can we boast about anyone's superior gifts or skills?

Why, rather than trying to build our own little kingdoms, we apostles have abandoned all that and have chosen humiliation, weakness, hunger, and even persecution as our lot. Imitate me in this, and get your priorities back in order. This is a warning. Unity in the family is so vital that, in God's own power, I will discipline you when I come unless you abandon your worldly arrogance!

God's Voice. That's how I like to study the Bible when trying to trace the thoughts of God and build my own mind by learning to think God's way. Surprisingly, studying to "hear God's Voice" in a personal meeting with Him has a different starting place than studying for understanding. It begins with our *feelings*.

Last February I was at Princeton for a short three-day course. During that time I had to decide about an invitation to return and teach a three-week summer session. I really wanted to cancel out and spend the time in Phoenix with my family. In my daily reading of Scripture these words from God appeared, and God brought them home to my heart. "Blessed is the man who swears to his own hurt and does not retract" (Ps. 15:4 NEB). God made it clear that this was His guidance for me, so I did spend most of June in New Jersey.

As I look over the Book of Psalms I see verse after verse that has ministered this kind of personal comfort and guidance to me. May 31 was a particularly discouraging day for one of the ministries in which I'm involved. That day the Lord reminded me, "The LORD is King for ever and ever" (Ps. 10:16). June 10 there was a hard decision to make. On that day this verse ministered to my need; "I keep the LORD always before me: because he is on my right hand I shall not be moved" (Ps. 16:8 RSV). On June 28 a number of choices were out of my hands and an important element of a ministry in which I am involved rested on the decisions of another. Would I trust my brother? "The earth is the LORD's and the fulness thereof" (Ps. 24:1 RSV) encouraged me to remember His sovereignty and His freedom to work in and through the lives of *all* His children.

In each of these situations there was (1) an awareness of personal need, and (2) an application by God the Spirit of what I read in Scripture to my heart. You and I can come to the Word of God daily to read only systematically. But we can also come "in touch with ourselves" and open up all our feelings and uncertainties to the Lord. We can resist the temptation to push the reality of our daily life aside and withdraw to Scripture as an escape. We can come, bringing all our life and our experience with us, and expect God to minister to us through His Word.

We have these same options as we come together in the family to meet with God. We can study very systematically, to understand God's thoughts. We can also begin with where we are personally, bringing our lives and our needs with us, to listen with our brothers and sisters for God's voice speaking directly to our need.

"Personal" Bible Study in the Family

One of the most serious misunderstandings of "personal" Bible study is that it can only be a private affair. We should read the Bible on our own. We will. And, because we are each important to God, He will speak to us. Personally, and individually. But don't let that lead you to the conclusion that we are always to study the Bible *alone*.

One of the most important truths of Scripture is the one we're looking at in this book. As Christians, you and I are no longer alone. When we entered that personal relationship with God in Jesus Christ, we were brought into a very real relationship with each other. Because God is our Father, we are now family, linked to every other child of His.

When I page through the New Testament I come to realize that what God shares with me is also to be shared with my brothers and sisters. I want to be open at all times to what God seeks to say through me.

This is what I was getting at when I said personal Bible study isn't strictly personal. It's not my private affair. I am to share what I'm learning with others, and I need to be in that close family relationship with others so that I can receive what they have to share with me.

There are so many evidences of this in the New Testament. Paul wrote to the Romans about his difficulty in going to visit them and said, "I myself am convinced, my brothers, that you yourselves are full of goodness, complete in knowledge, and competent to instruct one another" (Rom. 15:14). John spoke of the Holy Spirit whom we have been given and said we "do not need anyone to teach" us (1 John 2:27). We are not dependent on any single human teacher. Yet, because God has given each of us the gift of His Spirit to teach us, each of us can contribute to the growth of others. In Colossians our sharing is described this way: "Let the word of Christ dwell in you richly as you teach and admonish one another with all wisdom" (Col. 3:16).

We not only study the Bible for our own enrichment. We study so that we can minister to others.

Family Fellowship

How does the family approach the Bible when we gather in our fellowships? No, we don't argue about our doctrines—or fight about our convictions. Instead we come together, yearning to understand life as God does and eager to hear His living voice speak to the reality of our daily experience. Because we are a loving fellowship, we come with open lives.

I believe there should be a time when the church gathers to be instructed. But I also believe that we need to come together as Christians, in small loving fellowships, to share what God is teaching us with each other. We need to share feelings and needs, and listen as others communicate what God has taught them.

The goal of a fellowship, or family gathering, is not so much instruction as it is encouragement. The book of Hebrews puts it this way: "Let us consider how to stir one another up to love and good works, not neglecting to meet together, as is the habit of some, but encouraging one another, and all the more as you see the Day drawing near" (Heb. 10:24–25 RSV). We need to meet together, not to listen silently to a sermon, but to "encourage one another." The pulpit ministry is important to the life of a congregation, but it is not "all-important." There must be time set aside to share with the family what God has been saying to each of us personally. Time to "stir each other up to love and good works." Time to share the reality of God at work in our lives.

Nothing is more encouraging or more transforming than for God's people to share with one another what He is teaching them and then see His transforming Word bring growth and change.

Study in the Family

There are many ways and many settings in which we can study the Bible with brothers and sisters. Two persons can meet over lunch, and share what God has been teaching. A small group of eight or ten can study a common passage of Scripture and meet later to share. A small group can meet and be guided by special resources into a study–sharing process. Or skillful teaching in a Sunday school class can go beyond the facts about faith and help brothers and sisters explore their experience of God's truth in daily life.

There are many settings. But whatever the setting, each of us does need to share what God is saying to us with others. We need personal ventures into the Word of God. And we need to hear God's Word spoken to us by His family. Together we can learn to delight in the living, vital Word of our living God.

Allegiance

In a very real way, our allegiance to God is revealed by obedience to His Word. "He who loves me," Jesus said, "will keep my word" (John 14:23).

As family, we want to be a community of brothers and sisters who live in obedience to God's Word. Not because we have to. Not because others force us to conform to their ideas. But because we have come, through sharing together our understandings of God's Word and our own experience with the living voice of God, to a shared perception of what the Scripture says to us as family.

The Scriptures themselves say that no "scripture is of any private interpretation" (2 Peter 1:20 KJV). This may well mean that we can't take a verse or phrase out of the context of the whole of Scripture and understand it in isolation, but it also hints at the fact that we are not to rely on our own isolated interpretations of the Word either. We need to hear the voice of God through the filter of His family. We need to see how Christians down through the ages have held, with us, our common faith. We need to see how our brothers and sisters understand—and live—the words of God.

So we study together, in fellowship. We listen to each other, because we love each other. And as we listen, together, we sense a growing allegiance and loyalty to God.

Together we find fresh commitment to obey Him. Together, sharing each with the other, we move out to live as a whole family the exciting, vital, life-changing Word of the Living God.

Discovery 8

1. Read 1 John 3:1–10. Before looking at 1 John 3, review together the content of chapter 8. What for you was the single, most important concept introduced there? _____

_____

_____

_____

_____

2. Share what you have written with the others in your study group.

3. One John 3:1–10 focuses on *doing right*. We do not study the Bible just to know what God says, but so that through His Word He can lead us to do righteousness. Read the passage in 1 John carefully, and write down here phrases that help us understand God's reasons for focusing our attention on doing right.

a. _____

b. _____

c. _____

d. _____

e. _____

4. Discuss: What things about this Bible study group are most helpful to me and an aid to doing right?

5. Discuss: Is there anything about this study group that could be more helpful in encouraging me to do right?

6. Share: What role has Scripture played in my growth as a Christian up to now?

9

VERY PERSONAL PRAYER

"What really moved me," Gary was saying, "is that you people prayed and your prayers were answered."

Gary was looking back on his first weeks as part of a small fellowship group that met on Tuesdays in Charlie and Barbara's home. At the time Gary really thought of us as "you people." Before long it was "us!"

Gary had been raised a Catholic in New York. He's still a Catholic: part of a fine Catholic charismatic ministry in our city. But in the early days, none of his family knew Jesus in that very personal way we looked at at the beginning of this book. Gary wanted to. He was searching. But until he joined our small fellowship group he just hadn't known how.

Then he was drawn in along with his family by a fellowship of brothers and sisters who loved one another, despite great social, economic, racial, and religious background differences. In the context of God's loving family, Gary and his wife and brother all felt secure and loved. Before too long each established a personal relationship with God through trust in Jesus.

But I started with Gary's words about prayer. It was seeing

God answer prayer in that open, sharing, loving context of the family that impressed Gary with God's reality. This is another thing about living together as God's family. The intimacy of family life and family love permits us to open up all of our life to God and, together, seek His good gifts in prayer.

Intimacy

In the previous chapter I suggested that one way we're to approach Scripture is by exploring our own lives and then bringing the reality of what we feel, what we think, and who we are to the Word. Opening up our life to the scrutiny of Scripture is cleansing, healing, enriching . . . and life changing.

Much of what passes for Bible study in the church falls in the category of talking about ideas and concepts while carefully keeping our lives closed to God and to each other. When we study the Bible with our masks firmly in place we insulate ourselves and each other from the living voice of God.

But being a part of His family, where we are loved and where we belong, no matter what, frees us to become more open with God as well as with each other. In that atmosphere of freedom, God's Word comes to us powerfully and we respond to Him.

Now, in this chapter I want to suggest that a vital part of our life together as family is prayer: that the family relationship of love and intimacy frees us to experience prayer together as most Christians never experience it.

Gary's experience illustrates what I mean. He saw prayer answered, and recognized God's hand. These are some of the things Gary's group prayed about.

Pat had just been through a divorce, and was left with two small children. Her need? Her husband had always made all the decisions and had done everything for her. Now she was left with decisions and duties she was totally unprepared for.

Each week she had more frustrations, failures, and problems to share and to request prayer for. We watched as over the months God not only answered her specific prayers but helped her become a stronger, more self-sufficient person.

Pete struggled with many doubts and uncertainties. He was free to bring these to the group and not only had his questions discussed but his own inner turmoil bathed in prayer.

One couple in our group was involved in significant marital problems. He was a new Christian: she had not yet come to Christ. He blamed much of the problem on the fact that she was not yet a Christian. Yet he himself was responsible for many pressures on his beautiful wife, who had married one man some eight years ago and then found herself wed to a suddenly different person! For a time they took turns coming to the fellowship group. Each felt free in the context of love to share: each received support and encouragement and correction. Each was the object of much prayer. Because we knew intimately their feelings and needs we could pray with real fervor and wisdom.

Over the span of about a year God answered many of our prayers. Now, some four years later, this couple is happy together and growing in their relationship. The gal isn't yet a Christian. But he has been freed to love her without pressure, and leave the timing of her conversion to God.

Charlie struggled for a long time with the relationship between his faith and his business. He was able to talk about business problems, the kinds of choices he had to make, and the pressures he felt. As he shared over a period of months and was supported in prayer, the questions he raised were resolved and he found ways to live out his faith in God in the business world.

There were many others. There was sickness. There were jobs needed and found. There was the woman whose communication with her mother had broken down after her conversion. Again supportive suggestions and prayers transformed the situation.

In fact, one of the most exciting times of our sessions together was when we heard reports on the prayer requests each of us had written down. We shared our lives in that gathering of brothers and sisters as family. As a result we could focus our prayers on the real needs we each had.

This is the point I want to make. *Because we had learned to love each other so much we were free to open wide the doors of our lives to each other, so we could pray about the real issues in each of our lives.* The answers to prayer that moved Gary toward personal relationship with Jesus were *significant* answers to *significant* prayers.

I have been in many prayer meetings in the last twenty-eight years. Many of them are tragically superficial. Christians meet as strangers, holding back the real hurts and needs deep inside, and mention only the normal "prayer requests." Aunt Suzie is in the hospital. My son in the army needs prayer. There's political unrest in the country where the Bronson's are missionaries. Pray that our Sunday School will grow. I'd like everyone to pray for my neighbor who has cancer and isn't a Christian yet. And so on. The usual prayers are uttered, and the only insight we have into the reality of the lives of our brothers and sisters is the quiet voice that begs prayer for an "unspoken request." You can sense the pain in the voice. But sadly all you can do is ask God to meet the unspoken need and then go away, out into the cold, doubting that God has heard, or even that your prayers have been meaningful.

Well, there's *good news!* Prayer does not have to be like this for God's family! Here, in the warmth and love of brothers and sisters who care unconditionally, the inner hurts can be expressed. No one will condemn; no one will look down. Instead together we will look up to God, bringing the real needs we each experience to the Lord in confident prayer, and we will rejoice together as those prayers *are* answered.

And many, like Gary, will be drawn into our fellowships of love to discover the reality of a God who does answer the prayers of His children. A God who is real. A God who is known to be real because His children are real with Him and with each other!

Prayer

I suppose we shouldn't be surprised that prayer is a family affair. After all, we are taught in the Bible that Jesus has promised, "If two or three are gathered in my Name, there I am among you" (Matt. 18:20), and that if we on earth agree in prayer (come to a shared belief that we should make a particular request to God), we will have a positive answer (Matt. 18:19). We have many biblical examples—examples of how the apostles reported their experiences to the family, and all shared together in common prayer (*see* Acts 4:23–31; 12:1–10).

Certainly this doesn't mean that private, personal, individual prayer has no place in our Christian life. It has. But this does mean that we are not *restricted* to private prayers. We have been given the great gift of a family who will share our burdens and our joys, and with us they will bring both to God.

Another exciting thing about prayer is that it is based on our family relationship with God. Because God is our Father, we can bring our needs to Him freely. Because He is our Father, we can confidently share everything with Him.

This issue of confidence in prayer is an important one. Sometimes, in exploring books on prayer, we get the mistaken idea that praying is like negotiating an obstacle course. If we meet all the conditions and overcome all the obstacles, then we know our prayers will be answered. We tend to make prayer depend on what *we* do, not on God's goodness or graciousness or love—or His desire as a good Father to have fellowship with His own dear children.

One of Jesus' stories illustrates this point. It's found in Luke and it moves from the picture of a "friend" who finally answers a persistent petitioner simply to be rid of him, to the picture of a father who opens the door because of love. After all, if we expect human beings, who are tainted by sin, to love their children and be responsive to them, how much more can we expect God, who is wholly good, to love us and respond to our requests?

Look at Jesus' words:

> Suppose one of you has a friend, and he goes to him at midnight and says, "Friend, lend me three loaves of bread, because a friend of mine on a journey has come to me, and I have nothing to set before him."
>
> Then the one inside answers, "Don't bother me. The door is already locked, and my children are with me in bed. I can't get up and give you anything." I tell you, though he will not get up and give him the bread because he is his friend, yet because of the man's persistance he will get up and give him as much as he needs.
>
> So I say to you: Ask and it will be given to you; seek and you will find; knock and the door will be opened to you. For everyone who asks receives; he who seeks finds; and to him who knocks, the door will be opened.
>
> Which of you fathers, if your son asks for a fish, will give him a snake instead? Or if he asks for an egg, will give him a scorpion? If you then, though you are evil, know how to give good gifts to your children, how much more will your Father in heaven give [through] the Holy Spirit to those who ask him? (Luke 11:5–13).

God Is Father

Everything about our relationships within the family of God encourages intimacy. That intimacy is not only between us and our brothers and sisters; it is with the Father as well. Paul said in Romans that we've now received the Spirit of sonship and that now we approach God with the cry, "Abba." That's an unfamiliar word to most of us. But it wasn't to Paul's readers. In fact, the translators of the Bible couldn't quite bring themselves to put it into its English equivalent. You see, this was the first word that a young Hebrew child babbled as he learned to recognize his father. It means, literally, "Da da!" And then Paul explained, "The Spirit himself testifies with our spirit that we are God's children" (Rom. 8:15–16).

We are to count on God's unconditional love for us. We are to feel completely free to approach the One who is now our Father.

This freedom is sometimes difficult for us to feel. But in the family fellowship of brothers and sisters we can discover freedom with God as we experience it with each other.

In a way, that very freedom is reflected in the model prayer Jesus gave to His disciples in Matthew 6:8–13. He encourages them not to babble on as do pagans who think that they're heard because of their many words. Instead we trust God to know our needs even before we express them. In Jesus' model prayer, He gives us guidance as to how we are to come to God as Father. Look first at the prayer, and then let's think about its implications.

> Our Father in heaven,
> hallowed be your name,
> your kingdom come,
> your will be done
>   on earth as it is in heaven.
> Give us today our daily bread.
> Forgive us our debts,
>   as we also have forgiven our debtors.
> And lead us not into temptation,
> but deliver us from the evil one.

Our Father in heaven. Prayer flows out of our relationship. We approach God in the context of family assured of welcome, confident of love. The words "in heaven" remind us that any failings our human father may have had are not shared by God. His Fatherhood is a perfect one: His love is steadfast.

Hallowed be your name. We approach God in our relationship to Him, yet never unaware of who He is. He is God, and thus we respect Him and are confident that He is able to answer our prayers.

Your kingdom come. As family we are committed to the establishment of our Father's values and lifestyle. We seek to be, with each other and among the people of the world, expressions of His kingdom.

Your will be done on earth as in heaven. This thought also reflects the attitude of a child to the Father. In our relationship with God we see Him as the source and origin of our lives and values. We desire His will and are willing to be obedient to Him here on earth.

Give us this day our daily bread. So far in this model prayer we've focused on relationship. Now we're told we can live in daily dependence on God. Every daily need can be shared with God, who cares for each detail of our lives and who weaves His ultimate plan of good through our lives.

Forgive us . . . as we forgive. Forgiveness is by nature something like a door. If one side of a door is closed, the other will be too. If we open our lives to experience God's forgiving touch, we will be open to forgiving others. If we close ourselves off from forgiving others, we will never be able to believe that God forgives us and accept His grace.

Lead us not into temptation. One of the things that a small child recognizes is his own inadequacy. We are dependent beings. This aspect of prayer leads us to realize that in our relationship with the Father we are young children, who need His guidance.

What's the total picture? Again, we have the portrait of an intimate relationship between the Father and a child. The Father loves unconditionally and gives freely of His own strength, wisdom, and care and, in the process, meets all our needs. The child trusts the love of the Father, responds to His will, shares daily needs of every sort, and follows the guidance given him.

It is this lifestyle of dependence on a God who is truly our Father that we are called to experience together, as brothers and sisters, drawing close to each other as we grow in our intimacy with God.

Discovery 9

1. When you last prayed with other Christians, what did you share as a prayer request? _____

_____

_____

_____

_____

2. When you last prayed with other Christians, what did they share as prayer requests? _____

_____

_____

_____

_____

3. Share with each other the prayer requests you've jotted down. Then look together at the requests of Pat, Pete, Charlie and the others reported in the first part of the chapter. How

are the requests you jotted down *like* or *unlike* the ones in the chapter? What conclusions do you draw after hearing all report? Jot them down. _____

_____

_____

_____

4. Scripture says that believers are to "bear one another's burdens" (Gal. 6:2). What implications does this verse have for the topic discussed in this chapter? _____

_____

_____

_____

5. Divide into groups of six or eight. Share with each other, and spend time praying with and for each other.

10

ONE DEBT I OWE

This book is about God's family. It's about intimate personal relationships. It suggests that to be the people of God in today's world we are to live together—and experience Christian faith together—as family.

It's also about the rich and wonderful gift of love that God has given us in relationships. Because you are family, God has committed Himself to you. He is for you. He will always be loyal to you.

Because you are family, you belong with the rest of God's children. There are others God has given you to love you and be loyal to you, no matter what.

Because you are family, you're needed by your brothers and sisters. Through you God plans to enrich the lives of others in the family as you journey together toward Christlikeness.

Because you are family, you can grow so close to others and be so confident of their loyalty to you in Christ that you can share your life with them and receive their support and encouragement, their correction and care.

Because you are family and you realize that the basic identity of each Christian is in being a child of the heavenly Father, you have a basis for loyalty to others who differ from you. Differences of doctrine and convictions no longer need divide us, for we no longer demand conformity as the price of belonging. In the context of this kind of love, all of us can grow toward deeper understanding and a holier life.

Because you are family, if you or others stray into the practice of sin there is a loving discipline which will bring you back to God. You're not alone in your struggle to obey the Lord.

Because you are family, you can share in Bible study and prayer with each other. Your growth, your drawing closer to God, is supported by a closely knit community that is drawing closer and closer to the Lord with you.

Being family is not an option for us Christians. Living together as family is central to our experience of life in Christ. It is absolutely critical to your life as a Christian to build a family relationship with other Christians.

If you are fortunate, your local church is not just a fine institution, but also a family. Many local churches are. They encourage small fellowship groups and make other opportunities to build intimate personal relationships. Even if our local congregation is an institution and not a family, even if our church demands conformity and has lost sight of allegiance, you and I need to deepen our family relationship with other Christians. We *are* family, and we must, as God's dearly loved children, build a loving community of brothers and sisters.

Is Love Really Central?

This is one of the questions that may trouble us if we accept the Bible's teaching that being family is central to our lives as Christians. How will a focus on being family affect our commitment to holiness? Isn't keeping God's Law central? Or how will a focus on being family affect evangelism? Shouldn't reaching others with the Gospel be central? Or how will a focus on being family affect social concern? Shouldn't an active involvement in service and ministry be central?

When we raise these questions we find the Bible has a surprising answer. For those who say, "Concentrate on holiness," the Bible teaches that holiness begins with love. For those who say, "Concentrate on Evangelism," the Bible teaches that effective Evangelism is empowered by love. For those who say, "Concentrate on social concern," the Bible says that concern with human needs begins with love. Building family relationships of love and loyalty is foundational for all Christian growth and basic to a dynamic expression of Christian faith in our world.

Let's take just a few pages to study what Scripture says about the impact of love.

Holiness. "Let no debt remain outstanding," the Bible says in Romans 13, "except the continuing debt to love one another, for he who loves his fellow man has fulfilled the law." This surprising statement introduces us to an extended passage on God's family that we've already looked at briefly (Rom. 14–15). Here Paul argued that God's people were to wake up, shake off bondage to sin, and be clothed with Jesus Himself. "The hour has come," Paul said, to pull out of the mire of sin (see Rom. 13:11–14).

But to accomplish this transformation the Bible does not point us to Law. Instead we are pointed toward love! Why? Scripture explains:

> The commandments, "Do not commit adultery," "Do not murder," "Do not steal," "Do not covet," and whatever other commandment there may be, are summed up in this one rule: "Love your neighbor as yourself." Love does no harm to its neighbor. Therefore love is the fulfillment of the Law (Rom. 13:9–10).

Paul developed this same argument in Galatians. There he said, "You, my brothers, were called to be free. But do not use your freedom to indulge the sinful nature; rather, serve one another in love. The entire law is summed up in a single command: 'Love your neighbor as yourself.'"

Later, after pointing out the acts of the sinful nature and the fruit that God's Spirit brings to our lives, Paul added "against such things there is no law" (Gal. 5:13–14, 23).

What is the thought behind these teachings? Simply this. Law has always related to love, but negatively. God's Old Testament commandments speak out against the *unloving* acts which man committed against man. Law was not a positive force which motivated holiness. Instead Law stood as a warning and judgment against unholiness.

What does it take to motivate a truly holy life? Love. "Love does not harm its neighbor," "The entire law is summed up in a single command: 'Love your neighbor as yourself.'" *Love is the positive force that moves us to live a holy life.*

Actually, love for God and others is always associated with obedience. "Love the LORD your God, and walk in His ways," Moses said, linking love and obedience in the Old Testament (Deut. 11:22). And Jesus reinforced this concept in the New Testament when He said bluntly, "If anyone loves me, he will obey my teaching" (John 14:23).

No wonder then the emphasis in Scripture is on loving one another. "Be imitators of God, therefore as dearly loved children, and live a life of love, just as Christ loved us and gave himself up for us" (Eph. 5:1–2). We are God's children. We are family. And, like God, we are to live a life of love and loyalty.

Growth in holiness is directly related to growth in love.

Evangelism. The reality of love in our fellowship group, as that reality was expressed in our shared times of prayer, influenced Gary to become a Christian. But that's only natural. That's just the way God planned it.

We realize this when we look at what is called Jesus' new commandment. Just before the Last Supper, on the night before His crucifixion, Jesus shared many things with His followers. But the first instructions Jesus gave the disciples after Judas had left that evening were these:

> A new commandment I give you: Love one another. As I have loved you, so you must love one another. All men will know that you are my disciples if you love one another (John 13:34–35).

There are many things to note about the newness of this old injunction to love. It's new because a new relationship now exists between believers. In Christ we are family and the brother-sister intimacy open to us is unique. It's new because of the standard by which we are to measure love.

The Old Testament said, "Love your neighbor as yourself." Our love for ourselves was to be the standard by which we measured care for others. But now Jesus says we are to measure our love by the standard He set. "As I have loved you, so you must love one another!"

But the thing we want to note here is the new *outcome* of family love. "All men will know that you are my disciples if you love one another." The Good News of Jesus is made compellingly real by the reality of the family love between believers.

Of course, there must be more to sharing the Gospel compellingly than the evidence provided by family love. There must be the clear presentation of God's Word. In the earliest days of the Church there were additional evidences of signs and miracles. Yet the devotion of the family to "the apostle's teaching and to the fellowship" was a vital part of the early church's dynamic. "Every day they continued to meet together. . . . They broke bread in their homes and ate together with glad and sincere hearts." And "they enjoyed the favor of all the people" (Acts 2:42, 46, 47).

The love exhibited by the family was and is a vital part of our witness. First Thessalonians 1 traces the process in the lives of the believers at Thessalonica. The Gospel had come. The Gospel had been heard. The Gospel had been welcomed into their lives with joy, and then had rung out from them to others everywhere (1 Thess. 1:8). No wonder Paul said to the Thessalonians, "about brotherly love we do not need to write you, for you yourselves have been taught by God to love each other" (1 Thess. 4:9). Love is basic to the lifestyle of the evangelical church. Even so, Paul goes on to say, "You do love all the brothers throughout Macedonia. Yet we urge you, brothers, do so more and more" (1 Thess. 4:10).

Social concern. The Acts passages that describe the love that existed in the early church reveal their striking response to poverty. "All the believers were together," Luke wrote, "and had everything in common" (Acts 2:44). And, "there were no needy persons among them" for the possession of all were shared and "distributed to anyone as he had need" (4:34–35).

While there is no such thing as biblical communism, there are many clear statements of the fact that love means investing every kind of resource we may possess into our brother's lives. We cannot love and see our brother in need without acting to meet those needs (*see* 1 John 3:17). And James was very blunt in describing how true faith acts.

> Suppose a brother or a sister is without clothes and daily food. If one of you says to him, "Go, I wish you well; keep warm and well fed," but does nothing about his physical needs, what good is it? In the same way, faith by itself, if it is not accompanied by action, is dead (James 2:15–17).

Love moves us to involvement in the whole life and in every need of others.

It is true that this love is first of all a family kind of thing. "Do good to all people," Paul exhorted, "especially to those who belong to the family of believers" (Gal. 6:10). While there is a special obligation to love our brothers and sisters in the family, a love that allows us to hurt when we see others suffering extends beyond to all people. As Christ's love is nurtured in us and as we grow—in the family, and in the likeness of our Lord—we are moved to the kind of concern for others that James said makes true religion: "to look after orphans and widows in their distress and to keep oneself from being polluted by the world" (James 1:27).

One Debt

All this is behind Paul's statement in Romans about our obligation to one another. We owe each other one thing—love.

We must become in experience the family we already *are* in God's sight. This fact is behind the continuing exhortations we find throughout Scripture to love one another. Becoming a loving family simply is not optional: it is central.

As we develop a community of love, the visible expression of family adds impact to our witness to Jesus. As we develop a community of love, our shared commitment to one another and to God leads us away from sin toward holiness. As we develop a community of love, our growing sensitivity to human need leads us to meet the needs of brothers and sisters and to reach out to all mankind.

"Be devoted to one another in brotherly love," Romans says (12:10). Love is "the most excellent way" 1 Corinthians testifies (12:31). "Reaffirm your love" Paul exhorts in 2 Corinthians (2:8). "Serve one another in love," speaks Galatians (5:13). "Live a life of love" says Ephesians, "as God's dearly loved children" (5:2). I pray "that your love may abound more and more" adds Philippians (1:9).

Marching through the New Testament, each book adds its own testimony to the priority of love.

- "Over all these virtues put on love, which binds them all together in perfect unity" (Col. 3:14).
- "You have been taught by God to love one another" (1 Thess. 4:9).
- "The love every one of you has for each other is increasing" (2 Thess. 1:3).
- "The goal of this command is love," Paul writes about sound doctrine (1 Tim. 1:5).
- "Pursue righteousness, faith, love and peace along with those who call on the Lord out of a pure heart" (2 Tim. 2:22).
- "Teach what is in accord with sound doctrine . . . sound in faith, in love, and in endurance" (Titus 2:1–2).
- "I thank my God . . . because I hear about your faith in the Lord Jesus and your love for all the saints" (Philem. 5).
- "Keep on loving each other as brothers" (Heb. 13:1).
- "If you really keep the royal law found in Scripture, 'Love your neighbor as yourself,' you are doing right" (James 2:8).
- "Love one another deeply" (1 Peter 1:22).
- "Add to your brotherly kindness, love" (2 Peter 1:7).
- "Dear friends, let us love one another" (1 John 4:7).
- "I ask that we love one another" (2 John 5).
- "You are faithful in what you are doing for the brothers. . . . They have told the church about your love" (3 John 5–6).
- "Keep yourself in God's love" (Jude 21).

And so we see it clearly. Love is not optional. Love is central.

Love—growing intimacy in a family of brothers and sisters, is important to *you* in your own Christian life and growth. And love is possible! For God has placed you in His family, and you are *not* alone. Your brothers and sisters are all around you. So reach out and grow together in the fullness of God's love.

Discovery 10

1. Read 1 John 3:11–24.

2. Here are several quotes from this chapter. Talk together about what each one means. Then select one thought which seems "most important" to you.

- Love is the positive force that moves us to live a holy life.
- Love is the most compelling evidence of a living Christ.
- Love moves us to be involved in the whole life and every need of others.
- Love, and growing intimacy, in the family of brothers and sisters is important to *you* in your own Christian life and growth.

3. What is the significance of love among Christians (1 John 3:11–15)? _____

_____

_____

_____

_____

4. In what ways might love be expressed and received in the fellowship of Christians (1 John 3:16–20)? _____

_____

_____

_____

_____

_____

5. What is the relationship between loving one another and answered prayer in the Christian community (1 John 3:21–24)? _____

_____

_____

_____

6. In what ways have you experienced love in this group? List persons by name and jot down ways that they have communicated love to you.

NAME	LOVED ME BY . . .

11

LIVING THE LIFE OF LOVE

There's so much for each of us in living with other Christians as family. Our need for belonging is met. Our need for significance is met as we discover that our brothers and sisters need us to grow toward Christlikeness. We even learn to risk intimacy, gradually becoming convinced that others in the family truly are loyal to us. They love us so much they do not demand conformity as the price of acceptance.

Even great issues that have divided the church historically can be resolved when we approach them as family. Not that differences will disappear. Instead we learn that love can unify us in spite of differences of doctrine and differences of practice. And we've seen that the family is a place where Bible study and prayer take on expanded meaning for us.

All this is ours in the family of God. In the intimacy of deepening fellowship with our brothers and sisters, the foundation for vital Christian experience—and a vital church—is laid.

But how do we actually begin to live as a family? Let's look at some more pictures in Scripture that will help us see what pattern our life with others will take. By tracing the phrase "one another" through the New Testament we gain a clear and exciting picture of what life in the family is like. For it's that family, "one another" relationship, that Jesus' commandment involves. So let's trace that phrase through the New Testament together and look at the lifestyle described in its "one another" passages.

Romans 14:13. "Stop passing judgment on one another."

How many times have you thought of doing something—or not doing something—because of what others would think? Probably many times, because we have all learned that we live in a world in which people excuse themselves—and accuse each other. Somehow most people find it very natural to condemn others or to feel contempt for them. We learn quickly that we have to protect ourselves by responding to their expectations and pressures. The chances are that we've often felt that we're required to pass judgment on others!

How wonderful to be free from that kind of pressure. How wonderful to be able to consider only what God wants us to do, because we are convinced that our brothers and sisters won't misinterpret or judge our actions. We know that their love for us involves trusting us to follow Jesus, and that they will not place a bad interpretation on what they see us do.

*Romans 14:19.** "Let us . . . do what leads to peace and mutual edification."

The world is such a competitive place. We're told by everyone that we have to "look out for number one." Often our attitude toward others is linked to competition; we feel forced to gain an advantage over others if possible.

But in the family we leave all that behind us. I can care deeply about my brother's advantage and his growth, for I know that my brother is caring about mine. In this atmosphere

---

*While at times "one another" may not appear in the NIV translation quoted, it is present in other texts.

of mutual concern I find it possible to live in real peace with others. Every cause for strife is removed.

Romans 15:5. "May God give you . . . a spirit of unity among yourselves as you follow Jesus Christ."

So many things separate people from each other. There is status—the idea that some people rank higher than others, that some are superior because of their gifts or abilities or position. Often people try to outdo each other and show themselves superior. But in the family we're not trying to outdo each other or to build personal kingdoms. Instead we find unity in our mutual desire to follow Jesus.

How wonderful it is to have freedom from the nagging feeling that we must always measure ourselves against others and rank ourselves in relation to them. When God speaks of a "spirit of unity," He is promising us just this kind of freedom, for if we value each other as persons and if together we seek to follow only Jesus, we will have unity.

Romans 15:7. "Accept one another then, just as Christ accepted you."

In the family, we belong. It's comforting to know that our brothers and sisters won't examine us or set up an economic or social or educational or racial or religious or other kind of test for us to pass before we're accepted. The Bible says we're to accept each other "just as Christ accepted you," and that means without preconditions. Jesus knew our faults and failings and blemishes. He was not embarrassed by them. He welcomed us, and God calls us His own.

Now we've come to a family where we're accepted just this way: as we are. Where we learn to accept others just as fully and freely.

Romans 15:14. "I am confident, my brothers, that you are . . . competent to instruct one another."

Another version translates this "admonish." We are not left on our own when it comes to seeking to understand God's will. "Instruction" in this verse doesn't focus on content as much as on application: we have the opportunity to share insights and ideas with each other and, thus, to help each other find God's direction for our lives.

Being alone with a difficult decision isn't any fun. Sometimes we simply don't know what's best, or even what our options are. This promise of others to help us think through our problems is a very special one. The implication, that we can then help others too, is just as special.

1 Corinthians 12:25. "There should be no division in the body, but . . . its parts should have equal concern for each other."

Again we see the theme of unity, in that the people of God are not separated into different classes or categories. Some members of the family are not more significant than others. There is equal concern for each member, because we are each equally important in God's sight and to each other.

It's also important to realize that the family is not divided into "caring people" and "cared for people." Sometimes the biblical analogy of sheep and shepherds has been distorted to give the idea that the majority of Christians are helpless and hopeless nothings, who must be cared for by the stronger Christians. The Bible's picture is of a family in which each person is both competent and needy. Each can contribute to others and each needs contribution from others. The family is not divided into a "pastoral class" and a "laity class." We are one and have equal concern for one another.

Galatians 5:13. "Serve one another in love." God's picture of servanthood in Scripture is most beautiful. He shows us in the Old Testament that Israel was called to serve, but failed. Then the Servant–Messiah came and fulfilled God's will in caring for those He loves.

In the New Testament Christ identifies Himself as a servant, and calls us to live our lives serving others. We are to see

God's highest calling not in being the master of others so that they do our will, but in serving others so that their growth needs are met—which is God's good will.

How good it is to live in a family where others don't seek to manipulate us into serving their ends, but instead seek ways to serve us and help us grow.

Galatians 6:2. "Carry each other's burdens, and in this way you will fulfill the law of Christ."

Concerns, anxieties, doubts, uncertainties, troubles, needs, weaknesses, fear—all these are burdens that we bear. Because we are human beings living in a world that has been twisted by sin, there will always be pressures on us. And burdens to bear. But no longer are we forced to shut them up inside ourselves. Now, in the family, we can bare our burdens to brothers and sisters who care.

Sometimes bearing another's burden will simply involve listening and caring, and in this simple way, relieving the pressure. Other times bearing the burden will mean very practical action: meeting financial need, giving another person time, taking care of kids so a mother can have an afternoon free, and so on.

What's important is that in the Bible's portrait of family we find the freedom to share with each other the things that trouble us, we see the responsiveness of the family to the burdens revealed.

Ephesians 4:2. "Be patient; bearing with one another in love."

Another version says "forebearing," a word that means literally "putting up with." This verse recognizes the fact that even in the context of the family we continue to be imperfect—though growing—persons. We'll make mistakes. We'll say things that hurt or are misunderstood. And sometimes it will be necessary for us to put up with immaturity, anger, jealousy, selfishness, and other expressions of sin in

the lives of our brothers and sisters. But in the family there's
love enough to put up with the immature, and keep on caring
until they grow beyond the old ways which mark so many
lives apart from Christ.

Ephesians 4:25. "Each of you must put off falsehood and
speak truthfully to his neighbor, for we are members of one
body."

This passage isn't talking about truth versus lies. It's talking
about reality versus pretense. We're told that in the family we
are to put off insincerity and hypocrisy of every type, and be
ourselves with our brothers and sisters. We can speak the
truth freely because, loving as we do, we will always speak
the truth in love and be heard in love.

Ephesians 4:32. "Be kind and compassionate to one
another, forgiving each other, just as in Christ God forgave
you."

Again we see that the fallibility of members of the family is
recognized. We can face our failures, for our brothers and
sisters do not condemn. They don't look down on our weaknesses. Instead they're compassionate and forgiving, just as
God is.

Ephesians 5:21. "Submit to one another out of reverence
for Christ."

We've seen in earlier verses that in the family there is
equality: there is no division.

The family of God does not know of any such thing as a
ruling class. Instead we are ministers to each other. And we
are to submit to each other. Humility puts the interests and the
needs and the welfare of others first, and in this attitude of
mutual servanthood all the human distortions of au-
thoritarianism are put to rest.

Philippians 2:3. "In humility consider others better than
yourselves."

This picks up the same theme as Ephesians 5. We do not put

some on a pedestal so they can lord it over others. The family is marked by a humility which considers and honors the gifts and contributions of others above one's own. The whole concept of hierarchy is foreign to life and love in the family.

Colossians 3:13. "Bear with each other and forgive whatever grievances you may have against one another."

Again we have the picture of love between imperfect people, who find in their family relationship freedom to bear with and forgive.

1 Thessalonians 4:18. "Therefore encourage one another." Other versions suggest "comfort." The picture conveyed in the original Greek word is "to come alongside to support."

The content of this passage is about death and experiencing the fears of being separated from a loved one. God shares the good news that we will be together again. By reminding each other of this great truth and being there to affirm it to each other, we give encouragement and comfort.

We are to be sensitive to each other. We are to be by each other's side in need, with words of comfort drawn from our mutual faith.

Hebrews 10:24. "Let us consider how we may spur one another on toward love and good works."

There is a picture here of mutual accountability. We can be so concerned for another's success in following Jesus that we accept responsibility to stimulate him or her to take steps toward the goal.

There are many other "one another" pictures of life in God's family. Yet these few are a fair sample. They stand before us as a promise of the experience that can be ours in the family of God.

Too Ideal?

Many people would call this type of life together idealistic or utopian. They think that while it would be nice, the kind of life the Bible describes just isn't practical. Perhaps such a life could have been realized in an earlier time when people lived a simple agrarian life and had time to spend with each other. It would be wonderful, if it were not for the impersonal world we live in and the fact that our society runs counter to the family ideal.

How can we answer such a criticism? First by admitting that the Bible's picture of the church as family *is* ideal. The notion that Christians can live together in fellowship as a loving family is humanly impossible. But then, in spite of the fact that many of us have never experienced the kind of family love and intimacy that the Bible portrays, we affirm *anyway* that God's Word is true.

We *are* family. We have been born again in Christ into a new relationship with God. We have in our new birth been brought by God into a family of many brothers.

If God's Word is *true, then we can experience this reality*. We need not settle for superficial relationships in our congregations. We need not protect ourselves from others who may not yet understand what family means, because God's Spirit lives in each of His family, and they can learn and grow with us.

This really is the Christian perspective of life on this earth: We see the tangled web sin has made of life, but we affirm, even though we have not yet seen beauty and wholeness, that God can transform us individually and together and make His Word live! If at ninety-nine years of age Abraham "did not waver through unbelief regarding the promise of God, but was strengthened in his faith and gave glory to God, being fully persuaded that God had power to do what He had promised" (Rom. 4:20), then today you and I can reach out for family fellowship, and let God fill us with His power, so that what he promises about life with one another might become real to us.

Discovery 11

1. Read 1 John 4:7–18. Select from the chapter one of the "one another" verses that you believe is an especially important indication of love. Write it here. _____

_____

_____

2. Share with the others why you selected the verse you have written, and one or two ways that you have or would like to see the principle expressed in your own relationship with other Christians.

3. Work together in groups of six to complete each sentence three separate ways so that each sums up the teaching of the related passage:

1 John 4:7–8
Those who have experienced God's love . . .

_____

_____

_____

Love for one another . . .

_____

_____

_____

1 John 4:9–10
God's love is expressed most fully . . .

_____

_____

_____

1 John 4:11–12
God's love in Christ seems unreal to many, but . . .

_____

_____

_____

1 John 4:13–16
Evidence of our own personal relationship with God . . .

_____

_____

_____

1 John 4:17–18
We have no fear of judgment, because . . .

_____

_____

_____

4. God's love is the root and source of the love which Christians are freed in Christ to have for one another. What has happened in your own life since you became a Christian? Share with one another.

12

IMITATE THEIR FAITH

My wife and I have two sons. One, Paul, is now 23. The other, Tim, is 17, a senior in high school. One of God's best gifts to me as a father was the spacing of our children. I've had to travel far more than I like in my various ministries. And Paul, who lived at home while in college, was very close to Tim.

He wasn't a substitute father, exactly. But he was there, and he was a friend to Tim. By his maturity he was a stabilizing and supporting influence. Paul and Tim did many things together during Tim's adolescent years and, while I'd be wrong to suggest there was never any friction between them, Paul's consistent love for his brother and Tim's respect for Paul have been very important in Tim's growth.

In a real way, although they are equals in our family, Paul has been a leader that Tim has followed.

It's something like this in the family of God. It's right to stress the equality that exists between members of God's family, because God also stresses this in Scripture. We should learn to see each other not only as equals but as co-ministers, bearing each other's burdens, teaching and admonishing each other, contributing our gifts and service to help one another in our journey toward Christlikeness. In the family it's important not to fall into the trap of sacerdotalism: of setting up hierarchies of leaders, and treating them as though they were rulers ordained by God to take His place in our lives, rather than brothers.

At the same time, we realize that in the family of God there *are* those we are to respect as leaders. Just as Paul and Tim live together in my family as brothers, and yet Paul provides support and example as a leader, so it is to be in the family of God.

Not Rulers, but Servants

This is something that Jesus made very clear about leaders when he instructed his disciples. The Apostles themselves were not to be exalted over God's people as rulers. How much less then are leaders among us to be treated as, or to lift themselves up as rulers! Jesus said it this way:

> You know that the rulers of the Gentiles lord it over them, and that their high officials exercise authority over them. Not so with you. Instead, whoever wants to be first must be your slave—just as the Son of Man did not come to be served, but to serve, and to give his life as a ransom for many (Matt. 20:25–27).

Paul picked up this theme as he rebuked the Corinthian believers for forming their own "denominations" around human leaders like himself and Peter and Apollos. "Men ought to regard us as servants of Christ," he concluded (1 Cor. 4:1). For, as he pointed out at the beginning of his letter, neither Paul nor Peter were crucified for us. There is one to whom we have allegiance as leader: Jesus. While we have respect and appreciation for human leaders, we never forget that they are brothers and sisters rather than rulers.

The Christian leader always seeks to help individuals and the family toward personal responsiveness to Jesus, not to him or her. Like my son Paul with Tim, Christian leaders remain brothers. How then do leaders serve the family of God? In many ways.

With their gifts. Like other believers, leaders too have differing spiritual gifts. Some are teachers, some encouragers, some exhorters, some counselors or pastors. Service to them, as it does for the rest of the family, means using gifts that God has given for the building up of brothers and sisters.

With their lives. One of the repeated themes related to leadership is this. Leaders are persons who have moved ahead on their journey toward Christlikeness, and who can provide an example for others in the family to follow. "Let me be your example in this," Paul urged as he spoke to the Corinthians about dividing into cliques around different leaders. Paul's attitude of servanthood and humility is to pervade the body of Christ and bring our whole approach to leadership into perspective (1 Cor. 4:16).

Speaking to Timothy about his calling as a leader in the early church, Paul reminded him that he had intimately known Paul's life and teaching and was now to pay attention to his own life and teaching (*see* 2 Tim. 3:14). This is because it's the leader's task to "set an example for the believers in speech, in life, in love, in faith, and in purity" (1 Tim. 4:12).

Paul's words tell us much about the nature of Christian leadership. One implication is that the lives of leaders are to be well known. Intimacy and openness and the same kind of sharing that flows between members of the family is to exist between members of the family and those we recognize as leaders!

There is no room in Scripture for distance between leaders and others in the family. There's no room for exaltation and the wrong kind of respect. There is to be the right kind of respect. "Elders who direct the affairs of the church well are worthy of double honor," Paul says (1 Tim. 5:17). But it's the kind of honor given to a well-loved and respected brother or sister, whose gifts and godly life have earned the affection of the family.

Recognizing Leaders

How do we recognize those God has given to the family as leaders? The key is not found in their level of formal education, their ordination, or even in the kind of spiritual gifts they have to share with the brothers and sisters. The letters to Timothy and Titus in the New Testament help us recognize those whom God has appointed as leaders in the family (1 Tim. 3; Titus 1).

Look at some of the qualities the Bible describes:

above reproach	not conceited
temperate	respected by outsiders
self-controlled	not overbearing/or quick
hospitable	tempered
able to teach	not an alcoholic
not violent but gentle	a lover of good
not quarrelsome/or	holy
materialistic	disciplined
not a new convert	encouraging

What is striking about the list? Simply that it corresponds so clearly with the Bible's picture of the "one another" lifestyle. Look for instance at this picture in Colossians, from which we drew one of our "one another" pictures of family living.

> Put to death, therefore, whatever belongs to the earthly nature: sexual immorality, impurity, lust, evil desires and greed, which is idolatry. . . . You used to walk in these ways, in the life you once lived. But now you must rid yourselves of all such things as these: anger, rage, malice, slander, and filthy

language from your lips. . . . As God's chosen people, holy and dearly loved, clothe yourselves with compassion, kindness, humility, gentleness and patience. Bear with each other and forgive whatever grievances you may have against one another. Forgive as the Lord forgave you. And over all these virtues put on love, which binds them all together in perfect unity (Col. 3:5–14).

Looking at this very typical passage, we see a clear picture of how God's family lives out love. Comparing the qualifications given for leaders, we discover that *leaders are those who have already journeyed along this road and who can serve as examples of Christlikeness in the family.*

It's wrong to choose leaders and to follow men or women for their verbal skills or knowledge. It's wrong to choose as leaders and to follow those who by force of their personality dominate others. It's wrong to choose as leaders and to follow those who demand conformity and obedience. It's wrong to choose as leaders and to follow those who base their claim to recognition on one of society's ways of ascribing status.

In the family we seek out older brothers and sisters and recognize them by their maturity in Christ's way of love and servanthood. It is this kind of leader that we respond to.

Respecting Leaders

Christ's teaching to leaders stresses the fact that they are to accept the way of servanthood and to reject the world's approach of rule and authoritarian command. But the Bible's teaching to the family is that we are to respect and respond to those whom God has placed among us as examples of Christlikeness. Leaders are "worthy of honor," the Bible says. In the same paragraph in which Peter warns elders to be "as God wants you to be . . . not lording it over those entrusted to you, but being examples to the flock," he goes on to say to those younger in the faith, "be submissive to those who are older" (1 Peter 5:2–5).

One passage in Hebrews, clouded by the usual English translations, actually puts our response to leaders in clear perspective. Hebrews 13:17 is translated, "Obey your leaders and submit to their authority. . . . Obey them so that their work will be a joy, not a burden."

At first this seems to run counter to everything we've been saying. It seems we're not to be personally responsible to Jesus, even though He rose that He might be Lord (Rom. 14:9)! It seems that Christian leaders are to be "bosses" among the flock, and the rest of us are simply to do what they tell us.

But this is not what Hebrews says at all! The word translated "obey" means literally, "let yourselves be persuaded or convinced." A fair paraphrase would be, "Be open to the persuasion of your leaders."

The phrase translated "your leaders" is also of interest. While it's used to refer to princes and rulers, the original word means "to lead, or guide." Here we see the spiritual leader in the church as a person who has traveled along the road to godliness and is thus able to guide others.

A single Greek word is translated into the English phrase "submit to their authority." In classical Greek that word was used to describe soft yielding substances. The root meaning is not "give in," but "be disposed to yielding."

The whole exhortation focuses on the attitude which members of God's family are to maintain toward their leaders. Putting the thought together, we see it as it would have been understood by a reader of the Greek language in New Testament times: "In your relationship with those who are your leaders and guides to godliness, be sure you maintain a yielding disposition, and remain open to their persuasion. For they keep watch over you as men who must give an account.

Be responsive to them so that their work will be a joy, not a burden, for that would be of no advantage to you."

We *are* to respect and honor those we recognize as leaders. We honor them, because we see Christ being shaped in them. Because their example merits respect, we are always open to their persuasion. We know they love us, we believe they have proven their wisdom and godliness, and we are open to receive guidance.

What a different thing this is than the rigid rule normally conveyed by the term "obey." How beautiful it is that in the family respect does not mean fear, and honoring does not mean surrendering all personal responsibility!

For Christians, leadership means just what it means between my sons Paul and Timothy in our family. There is a loving relationship. There is sharing of lives and experiences. There is a respect and affection that leads the younger to be open to the thoughts and feelings and the suggestions of the one who's gone a little further along life's way.

That's What's Ahead—Family

Everything that we've described in our short exploration is ahead for you and for me with our brothers and sisters in the family of God.

It may be that you are already experiencing this kind of loving lifestyle with the Christians you know. It may be that you are just beginning to yearn for and reach out toward it. It may be that you're taking your first steps now, and that you're coming together with others for fellowship and to learn to be family.

Wherever you are in your journey as a Christian and in your experience of family fellowship, there's one thing both you and I can count on. God's Word is true, and God's Word about His family is true.

If what God says about our relationship with each other as

family is true, then *we can experience it as a reality in our own lives.*

How exciting to launch out in faith and become the family that we are.

Discovery 12

1. Read 1 John 5:1–12.

2. Spiritual leadership isn't necessarily an "office" or "position" kind of thing. It rests on the quality of the individual's life. Look over the characteristics of a spiritual leader as described in the chapter (p. 124). Can you think of two or three people in your study group whom these qualities describe? Jot down their names. _____

_____

_____

_____

3. What is the most important way that each has contributed to your life or demonstrated leadership? _____

_____

_____

_____

4. Leaders give of themselves to help others experience the great certainties of Christian life. What certainties can you discover about our relationship to God in 1 John 5:1–5?

_____

_____

_____

_____

_____

5. Because of our relationship with God, what experiences can we expect to have as we go on and grow in our Christian life (1 John 5:1–5)? _____

_____

_____

_____

_____

6. God's "testimony" about the Son is given both in Scripture and through others who know Him. What testimony, from the Bible or from one of the people you identified as a "leader," has helped you to experience new life in Christ (1 John 5:9–12)? _____

_____

_____

_____

_____

SUGGESTIONS FOR LEADERS

Chapter 1

The study you have chosen, *Our Life Together,* focuses on fellowship. Each chapter explores basic principles: your in-class studies focus on parallel teachings in the book of 1 John. An important goal for each study session is to (1) draw on concepts introduced in the chapter, (2) help your group discover them in 1 John, and (3) lead group members to share with one another. The sharing is especially important. God's Holy Spirit does minister to each believer through others. The supportive relationships that grow can be one of His most powerful stimulants to spiritual growth. This first week you will lead your group members to talk over items 1 and 2 of the discovery questions, and then divide into smaller groups of six or eight persons to complete activities 3 through 6.

1. On the definition of "fellowship" you may wish to read from pages 12–14.

2. Encourage as many as will to share here. Accept all suggestions. If some do not yet understand personal relationship with God, this understanding will come as they continue in your study group.

3–6. Divide the group and take part in one of them yourself.

Chapter 2

Before going on in 1 John, you want to help your group build an understanding of God's family, or the "fellowship" relationship that they can enjoy in Christ and that is the basis of John's teachings. This week you'll guide your group to return to the chapter, and to move together beyond the concept to actual steps that can be taken to live out the Bible truths studied.

Activities 1 and 2 will help define the warm and supportive climate that is to mark God's family. Reading again in the chapter will remind group members of the specific Bible passages that communicate this concept of the family of God. The discussion questions are to (1) lead to clearness about our relationship with God through Jesus, (2) lead to agreement that in Christ believers are brothers and sisters, and (3) by general discussion prepare for the group study on specific ways we can build relationships with others.

The important dimension of activities 4 and 5 is to become specific about what a person can do to reach out to others. There's no room to sit and wait for others to take the first steps when God's family is at stake. When we know things that we can do, we are more likely to respond to the promptings of the Spirit as He calls us to reach out to others.

Chapter 3

In this chapter your most important goal is to help each person discover and sense the fact that ministry takes place in a loving, family kind of interpersonal relationship. It is when we really do live together as God's own loving family that His Spirit works most freely among us.

After the sharing of activity 1 and 2, have each person divide the continuum lines under activity 3 in quarters, as below:

warm	37	5	1	0	cold

Make a composite, listing the number of those who have checked off each quarter. You will find a pattern like the one shown above appears when the numbers are added. The people who make an impact on others' lives are characteristically warm, close, have two-way communication in which they listen as well as talk, and communicate the feeling that they both care about the other person and know them well! It is the family context that God uses in His own building up of people.

For item 5, work together as a whole group. Review the chapter section and let your group members share their thoughts and ideas on each point. If you wish, take more time to look in-depth at the Bible passages quoted under each heading.

For your last study activity simply go around the circle and let each woman share what has been most meaningful to her personally in this particular study.

Chapter 4

The chapter shows that God's plan for us involves growth, and that His presence in our lives is revealed not by our sinlessness, but by the process of change within us. This means that for Jesus to be revealed, there needs to be some sharing of our weaknesses as well as our strengths as we build a fellowship relationship with others. Activity 1 is designed to help you be sure your class members have grasped this vital teaching before they move on to 1 John. In 1 John these same truths are related to relationship with God.

Direct Bible study in 1 John 1 is featured in items 3, 4, and 5. The discussion questions there help to apply the teaching of the passage.

Item 6 is for general discussion. It is to help your group realize that what John is saying has already been proven in their experience. We cannot come close to a person who hides his life from us.

The last item will help your group members move toward personal decisions related to the truths explored this session and in the text. Encourage your class members to speak in terms of themselves and their experiences, not in generalizations about "them" or "they."

Chapter 5

The class should be able to summarize the thrust of the chapter easily. While all other human associations are based to some extent on conformity, relationships in the body of Christ are of a family nature. We belong because of relationship with God in Christ, not because we agree with one another. Thus the teaching of 1 Corinthians 8 is especially important: love builds up. Claiming that we "know better" and insisting on basing relationships on agreement over doctrines "puffs up."

Items 2–6 directly explore a parallel passage in 1 John. There, speaking of fellowship, the apostle says that we are to focus on *obeying* the Word, not making tests of fellowship based on our *interpretation* of it. If we are obeying God, we will be in fellowship with the Lord, will grow in love, and will care deeply for our brothers. If we do not love our brothers, we are not walking in God's light.

Item 7 should be discussed at length, because this passage is linked with the content of the chapter. Time might well be best spent on personal sharing of the meaning of these truths for each person's life now.

Chapter 6

In the review of the chapter in item 1, your group should highlight the following points. Each individual is personally responsible to the Lord for his actions and choices. We are not to judge others or to look down on them for their choices. While there is freedom to be different and hold different convictions, there is no freedom either to impose our views on others or to flaunt our freedom in such a way that others are harmed.

Items 3 and 4 are designed to help your group see that even in their own lives "things" have not been the real issue. Instead our attitude toward things is the key to their meaning in our lives.

Items 5 and 6 return to reinforce this truth. Craving, lust of the eyes, and pride of possession all relate to our approach to things, and not to things themselves. God wants to purify us of worldly attitudes, and teach us not to judge by externals.

You should be able to get some sense of whether your class members have grasped these key truths as they share "significant personal learnings" as directed in item 7.

Chapter 7

Items 1–3 review material covered in the chapter. As you talk through the answers with your study group, be sure they see that discipline is limited to (a) believers, for (b) specific, habitual sin so defined in the Bible. Discipline is never to be used to force conformity, but to encourage a return to God.

Items 4–6 guide a study of parallel teaching in 1 John. Those who are not true believers will choose to leave the fellowship themselves, but they are *not* chased out (item 4)! Instead, because God's Spirit does live in believers, we can trust Him to help members of the Lord's family to distinguish between truth and falsehood (item 5). We need not be defensive or fearful. Instead we can love, knowing that love promotes growth, and that where there is true and deep love, the family of God will not be divided (item 6).

The last activity, item 7, will give your group an opportunity to think through and apply both the chapter and the 1 John passage. They should note that (a) discipline is for habitual practice of sin, not a slip; that (b) discipline is for what the Bible clearly identifies as sinful practices, not for doctrinal differences; that (c), and (d) are essentially true as stated.

Chapter 8

Take plenty of time for the sharing of what each person found the "most significant" concept in chapter eight (items 1, 2). In 1 John 3:1–10 many concepts are important. We are God's children now; with his heredity in us it is only appropriate we be like him. In fact, His presence means that we cannot keep on practicing sin as a way of life! God will work to purify us. The Bible becomes His living voice to us, helping us practice righteousness and become more like Him.

Discussion questions 4 and 5 are meant to both affirm strengths in your group and ways its members have helped each other follow Jesus, and to point up any weaknesses so they can be corrected.

Finally, in item 6, sharing will let more mature women in your group encourage others by relating personal experiences with God's transforming Word.

Chapter 9

The first three items are designed to help your group evaluate their own past experiences in praying with others. Some may have had positive experiences. Others may not. Encourage the women to talk about their experiences, and their own goals for prayer together in your study.

Item 4 helps focus on the clear implication of Galatians 6:2: we cannot bear each other's burdens until we bare our burdens to each other! This need not mean sharing in a large group: sometimes sharing and praying together is best done one on one, with an intimate friend. Suggest this possibility, but also express the desire that your group members might keep on growing together as a family of deepening trust and love.

Spend the largest amount of your time this week praying together in smaller groups. It's good to talk about prayer and understand prayer principles, but nothing can substitute for the experience.

Chapter 10

Begin by asking different members of your class to share about the meaning of the statements quoted in item 2. These summarize much of the thrust of this chapter.

Then move on to the direct study of 1 John 3:11–24, which stresses the meaning and importance of love in the Christian community. Talk through the passages together, but also be sure to reserve time for the important "affirmation" at the end of this session (item 6). Encourage your class members to jot down names of specific individuals in your group who have communicated love to them. Then, seated in a circle, let the women share one of the names and tell that person how God has used her to touch them with love.

Chapter 11

Item 1 permits your group to review in a very personal way the content of the text. The sharing (item 2) is something that you can do either in the larger study group, or in smaller groupings.

The Bible study (item 3) is best done in smaller groups, with applications drawn directly from the 1 John passage to complete the sentences. Item 4 may also be done in the smaller groups if you wish, or with the larger group reassembled.

Chapter 12

We grow in confidence in our relationship with God through the ministry of others and through the ministry of Scripture. Both are avenues through which the Holy Spirit gives His unique testimony.

Items 2 and 3 help your group members focus on others that God has given them confidence in. It would be helpful to take time to share the names the women have jotted down, and how each one written down has ministered to them.

For items 4 and 5 take time to talk about and list several certainties from 1 John 5:1–5 and to explore experiences that we can expect to have. For instance, the passage tells us that we *have* eternal life in Christ. In the future then we can expect to grow, for all living things grow and mature.

The final item (6) is one in which you will want to encourage many to share. Expressing truths that have become a reality—a certainty—will help each class member realize in a fresh way how God has been active in her life.